A History of Lighthouses

A HISTORY OF LIGHTHOUSES

Patrick Beaver

Anythin' for a quiet life, as the man
said wen he took the sitivation at the
lighthouse.

Sam Weller

THE CITADEL PRESS
SECAUCUS, NEW JERSEY

First American edition, 1973
Copyright © 1971 by Patrick Beaver
All rights reserved
Published by Citadel Press, Inc.
A subsidiary of Lyle Stuart, Inc.
120 Enterprise Ave., Secaucus, N.J. 07094
Manufactured in the United States of America
Library of Congress catalog card number: 72-95414
ISBN 0-8065-0368-8

To Anthony and Sally

Contents

Illustrations

Preface

There can be few of us who, upon seeing the friendly glow of the light-house from ship or from shore, have not warmed a little at this rare instance of mankind's better instincts. The lighthouse has long been a favourite subject for romance and yet, at a time when fiction is giving way to fact in the demand for books, there is comparatively little material on the subject of sea-lights available to the general reader. The intention of this book is to trace the development of the lighthouse from its origins as an open fire on the beach to the complex structure it is today, and to relate how lighthouse designers and builders have, over the centuries, responded to challenges of ever-increasing complexity as the trade and the sea-routes of the world multiplied.

As the number of lighthouses in existence now exceeds 50,000[1] it will be appreciated that my task has been mainly one of selection. The light-houses I have described were chosen for one or both of the following reasons: because they each mark a major development in the science of pharology or because the drama of their building is worth relating. There-fore, it should not be thought, because I have made scant reference to the coastal lights of, for instance, Australia and none at all to those of South Africa, that these coasts are ill-served with beacons. On the contrary, they are as adequately lit as any in the world and their lighthouses are exceptional for the fine quality of their architecture; it is because the majority of these light stations are on shore or on islands that they cannot compare with such works as Eddystone, Minot's Ledge or Heaux de Bréhat.

On behalf of the publishers and myself I would like to thank the following individuals and institutions for the willing help they have given me: the Corporation of Trinity House and in particular its officers, Messrs N. F.

---

[1] This is a safe estimate and does not include those built on the inland seas of America and Russia or upon the great navigable waterways. These would amount to at least another 10,000.

Matthews, G. S. Thomson and S. C. Isbel; Messrs Christiani and Nielson Limited; the National Swedish Board of Shipping and Navigation; the Embassy of the Dominican Republic in London; the Hawker Siddeley Group of Companies; the Central Electricity Generating Board; Miss Susan Bruce; Miss Jane de Wardener; Mr D. Alan Stevenson, Mr C. J. Antonakis, B.Sc.(Eng.), A.C.G.I., F.I.C.E., Mr James Napier, and Mr Douglas FitzPatrick.

I would also like to thank my wife for the great amount of time she spent in checking, correcting and retyping the manuscript.

A History of Lighthouses

I

The Need for Sea-lights

MAN IS A persistent and tenacious creature. In his constant struggle with the forces of nature he has always been faced with challenges and has never hesitated to take up the gauntlet. When fishermen first ventured out to sea to obtain food the concept of the sea-light was born, for it was natural for their friends on the shore to light fires to guide them home when wind, weather and tides prevented return before nightfall. From this simple act of humanity grew the lighthouse system of today—a highly specialized branch of engineering involving architecture, optics, radio, electronics, acoustics and oceanography, to name but some of the sciences now employed in making the seas safe for shipping. On all the world's trade routes lighthouses will be found performing their age-old service to mankind—protecting ships and the lives of those sailing in them.

The hazards marked by the world's sea-lights were probably given their names by early navigators and this would account for the sinister and forbidding sound of Eddystone, Skerryvore, Dhu-Heartach, Danger Point, The Lizard, Coffin Island, Wolf Rock, Minot's Ledge, The Graves, Muckle Flugger, One Fathom Bank, Race Rock, Foul Island, and False Point. It is difficult to imagine what it was like to be a sailor in the days when these hazards, and thousands like them, were still unlit. The early mariners, with their inaccurate charts, sea surveys and 'sailing instructions' and with inadequate navigational instruments, depended mainly on what could be seen. At night storms and fogs upset the calculations of navigators who received their first intimation of danger perhaps from the sight of white water which almost invariably meant doom, while of the submerged reef he might have no knowledge at all until it announced its proximity by tearing out the bottom of his ship.

There can be no doubt that the lighthouse is the greatest boon ever to be bestowed upon navigators. By means of its signal, be it a light, a bell, a siren or a radio signal, ships can now move along the most treacherous coast at night or in a fog with perfect safety. The Cornish coast, probably the most fearsome in the world, has taken its toll of ships for thousands of years. Its hazards are so numerous and formidable that it seems incredible that it was regularly navigated for some 2,000 years before it was adequately lit. In approaching the Scilly Isles from the Atlantic, the modern navigator's first landfall is the powerful light of Bishop's Rock, four miles to the west of the Scillies; then, if making for Plymouth, he will pass Penninis light and the isolated Wolf Rock light. He will then pick up the Lizard light on the mainland and then the light that warns him away from that grim graveyard of shipping, the Eddystone Rock. On the Bristol Channel route the first light to be seen after Bishop's Rock is the one on Round Island, and as this drops astern the Sevenstones lightship comes into view. Then follow the lights on Longships' Reef, Pendeen, Trevose, Hartland and Lundy Island.

Lighthouses fall into three general categories—main lights marking shoals, rocks in the sea and landfalls; coastal lights marking headlands; secondary lights marking hazards which lie near the main shipping routes. The lights themselves are divided into six ratings, or orders, the most powerful being lights of the first order. Lights that do not flash are known as fixed lights and all early lighthouses were of this type. The light merely indicated that a danger existed but gave no information as to its nature. Later the principle was introduced of turning off the light at definite intervals thus making it easily identifiable. This shutting off of an oil-lamp was contrived by revolving the lens or a screen, or by lowering a cylinder over the light. The number of variations obtainable by this system is, of course, infinite but they fall into the main categories shown opposite.

Alternating Light

The brilliancy and range of a sea-light depend less on the light source, which may be an incandescent mantle or an electric lamp only slightly larger than an ordinary one, than upon the magnifying powers of lenses or mirrors. Lamps are described by the nature of the optical system involved, there being three types: catoptric, in which the light is reflected and concentrated by means of a metallic reflector; dioptric, in which the light is passed through glass lenses and prisms which concentrate it into parallel beams; catadioptric, which combines, as the word implies, both these methods.

The range of a light is dependent upon two factors apart from weather conditions—brilliancy and the height of the lantern above sea-level. If the eye-level height of the navigator on the bridge of a ship is, for instance,

TABLE OF LIGHTS

Lights; the colour of which does not alter when viewed from a given position	Characteristic phases	Lights which alter in colour when viewed from a given position
Fixed	A continuous steady light	Alternating
Flashing	(a) Showing a single flash at regular intervals, the duration of light being always less than that of darkness (b) A steady light with, at regular intervals, a total eclipse, the duration of light being always less than that of darkness	Alternating flashing
Group flashing	Showing, at regular intervals, a group of two or more flashes	Alternating group flashing
Occulting	A steady light with, at regular intervals, a sudden and total eclipse; the duration of darkness being always less than, or equal to, that of light	Alternating occulting
Group occulting	A steady light with, at regular intervals, a group of two or more sudden eclipses	Alternating group occulting
Fixed and flashing	A fixed light varied, at regular intervals, by a single flash of relatively greater brilliancy. The flash may or may not be preceded and followed by an eclipse	Alternating fixed and flashing
Fixed and group flashing	A fixed light varied, at regular intervals, by a group of two or more flashes of relatively greater brilliancy. The group may or may not be preceded and followed by an eclipse	Alternating fixed and group flashing

25 feet above sea-level, the horizon will be 5·7 nautical miles away, while at 120 feet the distance to the horizon will be 12·56 nautical miles. The effective range of a light 120 feet above the sea, therefore, would be 18·26 nautical miles when observed by our navigator. The following table may be of interest:

Feet above sea-level	Distance to horizon in nautical miles
5	2·5
15	4·44
25	5·7
100	11·7
120	12·56
150	14
200	16

Lighthouses often have to be built on sites that are difficult of access—on submerged shoals, sunken rocks, precipitous headlands or wave-swept rocks, and it is under these conditions that the true qualities of the engineer are called for. The type of lighthouse and its siting will be dictated to the designer by local conditions, no matter how impossible it might appear at first to build upon a particular spot. To build a lighthouse on submerged sands means that the engineer must sink his foundations to a solid level, while to build on a wave-swept rock may involve many dangers, known and unknown.

The building of lighthouses under such conditions as these forms as difficult a task as often falls to the lot of the patient and ingenious engineer; and to fight successfully such battles with the wild forces of nature, while the pessimists around are pleasantly telling you that you will never succeed, and while your best efforts seem again and again defeated—to fight such battles and win such victories exhibits accomplished skill and determined courage in no common degree.[1]

Lighthouses may be divided into two classes, those built on rocks, shoals, islets or in other places exposed to the sea, and those built on land. Of the former class, which we will call 'wave-swept' towers, there are the following types: masonry and concrete buildings; 'skeleton' structures of openwork steel or iron built on piles or other foundation; cast-iron plated towers; towers or lantern-houses built on caisson foundations.

Masonry towers are usually preferred where the natural foundations are solid, although many have been built on caissons sunk into the soft sea-bed; but the ideal, of course, is the tower built upon the rock it guards, for it follows that wave-swept rocks must be very hard indeed, otherwise the action of the sea would have worn them away ages ago. In designing

[1] From *Lightships and Lighthouses* by F. A. Talbot.

masonry towers for wave-swept situations certain basic principles are followed:

1 The centre of gravity is kept as low as possible.

2 The mass of the building superimposed at any horizontal section must be sufficient to prevent its displacement by the combined forces of wind and weather.

3 Ideally the structure should be circular to afford the minimum resistance to wind and wave.

4 The base of the tower should be cylindrical to resist the horizontal thrust of the waves while the upper portion should be a curve receding at such an angle that the waves will be carried upward and thrown back on themselves, thus saving the tower from the full force of the blow.

5 The outer surface should be smooth and as free as possible from projections.

6 The height of the tower should, apart from considerations concerning the effective range of the light, be sufficient to keep the lantern clear of water or spray.

It can be seen from these considerations that a wave-swept lighthouse is a marvel of ingenuity and that it needs to be, for the forces against which the lighthouse engineer pits his wits are well-nigh incredible. The forces can be shown in table form:

Wind velocity in m.p.h.	*Pressure in lb. per sq. in.*	*Description*
1	·005	Gentle breeze
15	1·007	Brisk breeze
50	10·000	Wind
80	26·000	Hurricane
108	46·000	Destructive hurricane

Skeleton structures are suitable for supporting lights on soft or insecure bottoms—on sandbanks, coral reefs and shoals while cast-iron plated towers have been erected in places where scarcity of stone or of skilled labour has prohibited the building of a masonry tower.

Lighthouse administration, which was once a highly profitable form of private enterprise, is now carried out by the government of the country concerned and the money to maintain the service comes from taxation. The one exception to this rule is the lighthouse service of England, Wales, the Channel Islands and Gibraltar, the authority of which is the Corporation of Trinity House which, apart from erecting and maintaining navigation lights, collects light dues from all vessels using ports within its authority, the money received being used to finance its work.

The Corporation of Trinity House is unique in many ways. No organization connected in any form with ships and shipping possesses such a romantic past, while being concerned primarily with such a practical matter as the safety of ships and sailors. Unfortunately it is not possible to trace the entire history of Trinity House; too many gaps have been made in its records by fires and other mishaps—in particular the Civil War, the Great Fire of London (1666), another fire in 1714 and, most disastrous of all, the fire-bombing of 30 December 1940.

Although the origin of the Corporation cannot be established with certainty it probably developed from the Trinity Guild formed by Archbishop Stephen Langton in the thirteenth century. Functioning as a charity for the benefit of seamen and their families, the Guild owned a hall and almshouses at Deptford. Langton was closely connected with maritime matters and it is likely that the Guild was formed for other purposes apart from charity—one of them being to check the pillaging of wrecked ships on the English coast. The archbishop would have been acting in his own interests by so doing, for the ecclesiastical authorities owned certain rights of wreck.

The business of looting wrecked ships had been carried out by coast-dwellers from time immemorial and no doubt it would flourish today if given the opportunity, although doubtless modern plunderers would cast a less callous eye on the unfortunate passengers and crew than did the wreckers of earlier times. Ancient Greek and Roman coast-dwellers took over all wrecks that came their way as a matter of right and they sold not only the cargoes of the ships but the crews, who fetched a good price on the slave market. Even up to the sixteenth century there were inhabitants of some British coasts who, descending upon a wrecked ship, killed the crew before taking the cargo, it being considered that survivors of wrecked ships brought bad luck with them.

In 1514 the Trinity Guild (or, to give its full title, 'The Master, Wardens and Assistants of the Guild, Fraternity or Brotherhood of the Most Glorious and Undividable Trinity and of Saint Clement in the Parish of Deptford Strond in the County of Kent') was granted a charter of Incorporation by King Henry VIII and, in spite of its strongly religious character and unmistakably Catholic title, it was left unmolested by the king at the time of the dissolution of the monasteries. When the boy King Edward VI came to the throne, however, his advisers cast greedy eyes on those religious guilds that had escaped the attention of Henry, and so the Brethren quickly changed the name of the Guild to 'The Corporation of Trinity House on Deptford Strond', thus obtaining the confirmation of their charter by Edward and subsequently by Elizabeth. In 1565 an Act of Parliament empowered the Corporation to erect 'such and so many beacons, marks and signs for the sea in such place or places of the sea-shores and uplands near the sea-coasts or forelands of the sea whereby the dangers may be avoided and escaped and ships the better come unto their ports without peril'.

Despite these powers the Trinity House Brethren did not build their first lighthouse for another 125 years and this is not surprising when the scope of their other activities during the period is considered. In addition to its charitable works the Corporation was the examining body in navigation and mathematics to the boys of Christ's Hospital; it supervised the building of piers and harbours, trained and licensed maritime pilots, gave expert advice on the design of warships and even, on occasions, organized press gangs. In 1680 it built its first lighthouse—in the Scilly Isles—and by 1801 it controlled twenty-three navigation lights, one of which was the Eddystone. In 1836 an Act was passed by Parliament that compulsorily transferred all English and Welsh lighthouses to Trinity House on condition that the private owners were compensated.

Trinity House is now responsible for about ninety lighthouses as well as thirty light-vessels and nearly seven hundred buoys, over half of which are lighted. Some local and harbour authorities establish and maintain their own sea-lights but these come under regular inspection by Trinity House whose sanction must be obtained before any changes are made.

Today's light dues are levied on a scale and in accordance with the rules laid down in an Act of Parliament of 1898. The following list shows how the 1898 rates compare with those currently (1971) operating:

		Sailing Vessels	Steamers
Home-trade voyage	1898	1d per ton	1½d per ton
	1971	6·3d per ton	9·45d per ton
Foreign-bound voyage	1898	2¾d per ton	2¾d per ton
	1971	1s 2·175d per ton	1s 5·325d per ton
Cruise voyage	1898		8d per ton
	1971		9·6d per ton
Tugs and pleasure yachts	1898		1s 0d per ton p.a.
	1971		6s 3·6d per ton p.a.

The liability of ships to light dues is limited in the case of home-trade ships to ten voyages in any one year and in the case of foreign-going ships to six voyages in a year. The light dues collected by the Corporation currently amount to £6 million per annum.

It must be said of Trinity House that once in the lighthouse business they made a magnificent job of it, and well before the end of the century the British coast was the best lighted of any. But the nineteenth century was the golden age of lighthouse building all over the world, and as towers were built in more and more inaccessible places lighthouse building emerged as a highly specialized branch of engineering, producing such men as Walker, Douglass, Alexander, and the Stevensons[1]—

[1] The Stevenson family of lighthouse builders is not to be confused with the railway Stephensons.

master craftsmen whose calibre was equal to that of any of their more famous colleagues. The Industrial Revolution, in producing a vast increase in the supply of consumer goods, was compelled to produce the steamships to carry them and, as the speed, size and number of these ships increased, it became desirable to build more lighthouses with more powerful lights.

The age that produced the *Great Eastern* also produced, among others, Skerryvore and Bishop's Rock lighthouses, and by 1880 there were no fewer than 3,500 light-stations operating throughout the world. Lamps, reflectors and lenses were all steadily improved upon during the course of the nineteenth century, and as early as 1859 an English lighthouse had been supplied with electric light. The engineers of that restless and energetic century who did so much to light the sea hazards of the world were at their supreme best in building the classic—one could almost say the 'archetype' of the lighthouse: the slim granite tower springing from an isolated wave-swept rock or from the sea itself. Because of the great forces they have to withstand, from wind and storm, sea and tempest, these are essentially functional structures, built solely for strength and for showing a light. As a consequence there are little or no architectural embellishments in wave-swept towers. In an age when ships, forts and even guns were elaborately decorated and embellished, little in the way of aesthetic consideration was allowed to intrude upon the purely utilitarian approach to the designs of these towers. This lesson was learned from the fate of the wave-swept tower built by Winstanley on Eddystone Rock in 1696–8 (Plate 1a). This fantastic building with its cupolas, eaves, and balconies was treated by the sea with the contempt it deserved and was swept away one night, probably by a single wave, so that no trace of it remained. Yet the wave-swept towers, supreme examples of pure functionalism with their delicate proportions and their hyperbolic lines, possess a strange, remote beauty. They conjure up all that is romantic and all that is sinister about the sea; standing lonely and isolated with the waves dashing vainly at their feet, their high crests of light flash far and wide over the dark water.

Each wave-swept tower performs two functions in addition to its primary one. It stands as a monument to the skill, determination and courage of the men who built it, and as a memorial to those whose graves lie around. For it was their tragedies that called the lighthouse into existence.

2

Ancient Sea-lights and Towers

WE HAVE SEEN how primitive off-shore fishermen would have been guided home at night by fires lighted on the beach. This early use of fire beacons is confirmed in the legend of Hero and Leander, for we are told how Leander, having fallen in love with the priestess Hero, swam the Hellespont every night in order to see her—she burning a light to guide him across. One night a storm put out the light and Leander was drowned. Another legend attributes the first lighted sea-beacon to Hercules who, having donned the shirt of Nessus, in his agony tore the flesh from his own body. Unable to stand the pain, he built himself a funeral pyre by the sea and threw himself upon it. At Thasos, Smyrna and in Italy he was known as the saviour, i.e. protector, of voyagers. Still another story tells how Nauplius wrecked the Greek fleet by exhibiting false lights on the shore. This story shows that the craft of wrecking was also practised in ancient times in much the same way as it survived into the nineteenth century. No mention of beacon fires can be found in the Bible—but the Jews never were a maritime people.

It is known that in the seventh century the Phoenicians, then the only maritime nation in the world worth consideration, made regular voyages to the Scilly Islands and to Cornwall in search of tin. These fearless and patient navigators, having to sail out of the Mediterranean into the North Atlantic, making their way down the Iberian coast and across the Bay of Biscay before negotiating the fearsome Cornish coast, must have been aided by some shore lights at night if only to guide them safely past the barrier of isolated rocks which guard the Scilly Islands. The present light-house at Corunna is built near the site of a Phoenician beacon.

The earliest-known lighthouses were built by the Sybians and Cushites of Lower Egypt. These towers were, like early bridges, used as temples and held in great reverence by seafarers who made sacrifice in them. It is supposed that the inner walls of these buildings were engraved with charts and that the light-keepers were priests who also taught seamanship, pilotage, astronomy and hydrography. The lights were provided by wood fires that burned in iron braziers in the form of interlaced dolphins suspended from the towers with long poles.

Lesches, a minor poet who flourished around 660 B.C., tells of a lighthouse on the promontory of Sigaeum in the Troad and this seems to be the first lighthouse that was regularly operated. It was strategically situated to guide ships to Troy, Hellespont, the Sea of Marmora, the Bosphorus and the Black Sea.

Legend has it that the Colossus of Rhodes was a lighthouse in so far as the figure of Apollo held a torch aloft upon which a fire was lit at night to guide ships into harbour. The figure was about one hundred feet high, made of bronze and, whether or not lit at night, it must have been a seamark, standing as it did with legs astride the entrance to Rhodes harbour. Built in about 300 B.C. by a pupil of Lysippus, the greatest of Greek sculptors, it stood for eighty years before being overthrown by an earthquake.

The renowned Pharos of Alexandria received its name from the island on which it was built and there can be no doubt that it was a lighthouse. Built on a base 100 feet square, it was 450 feet high and carried an open fire that could be seen for twenty-nine miles. The building, which was started in 261 B.C., taking nineteen years to complete, ranked as one of the seven wonders of the ancient world, thus implying that it was comparable in size with the Great Pyramid. The very magnitude of this structure indicates that earlier lighthouses existed for such a huge and costly project would not have been undertaken if the value of permanent sea lights had not been appreciated. No other lighthouse in history rivals it in size or in its 1,500 years of service. Although this great structure has been variously ascribed to Alexander the Great and to Cleopatra it is fairly certain that it was built by Ptolemy II and that the architect was Sostratus of Gnidus. It is said that Sostratus, wishing, understandably, for his name to be perpetuated as the builder of one of the world's seven wonders, inscribed on the finished building the following legend: 'Sostratus of Gnidus, son of Dixiphanus, to the Gods protecting those upon the sea'. Realizing, however, that this inscription would not please his master, he covered it with cement and wrote in it the name of Ptolemy, knowing full well that it would not long outlive the king: eventually it would wear off and reveal the permanent inscription that gave credit where it was due. This simple ruse seems to have worked for, writing about the tower some hundreds of years later, Pliny the Younger comments: 'I cannot but note the singular magnanimity of kind Ptolemy, who permitted Sostratus of Gnidus to grave his own name in this building.'

In the thirteenth century the tower was visited by the Arabian geographer Edrisi, and from his description of it, it appears that despite its 1,500 years it was almost as good as new:

This lighthouse has not its equal in the world for excellence of construction and for strength, for not only is it constructed of a fine quality stone, called 'kedan', but the various blocks are so strongly cemented together with melted lead, that the whole is imperishable, although the waves of the sea continually break against its northern face; a staircase of the ordinary width, constructed in the interior, extends as high as the middle of the structure, where there is a gallery; under the staircase are the keepers' apartments; above the gallery the tower becomes smaller and smaller until it can be embraced by the arms of a man. From the same gallery there is a staircase much narrower than the tower, reaching to the summit; it is pierced by many windows to give light within and to show those who ascend where to place their feet. At a distance the light appeared so much like a star near the horizon that sailors were frequently deceived by it.

It is of interest to know that the method used by Sostratus of 'cementing' his blocks of stone together with melted lead was the same used some 2,000 years later when Rudyerd built the second Eddystone lighthouse.

Descriptions of the exterior vary considerably, but it is likely that the tower consisted of three tiers like a stepped pyramid. The bottom tier was of white marble and square in shape, the second tier was octagonal and the uppermost circular. The whole building was elaborated with pillared galleries, and on the summit of this remarkable building a wood fire was kept burning continuously, thus providing a light by night and a column of smoke by day. How the insatiable appetite of the signal was satisfied is a mystery for if, as we are told, this large fire was maintained for 1,500 years it must have consumed whole forests.

So renowned was this lighthouse that the word Pharos became generic for all sea-lights in the world. The Latin word for lighthouse is *pharus*, in Italian, Spanish and Portuguese, *faro*, in French *phare* and the word *pharos* lingered in the English language up to the seventeenth century. The science of lighthouse engineering is still known as pharology. Sostratus' tower withstood the ravages of weather, sea and time until well into the thirteenth century when it was toppled by an earthquake; its ruins were still visible in 1350. Empires came, went and were forgotten through a millennium and a half, but Ptolemy's light burned on.

The old authors make but scant reference to lighthouses and this implies that such buildings were numerous enough to be considered commonplace. But however numerous they may have been, no trace of the lighthouses of the ancient world survives. This is reasonable when we consider that lighthouses are usually situated in exposed places, subject to wind and storm and the ravages of the sea. In addition, those existing in ancient times were invariably placed near harbours and other strategic points where they were liable to enemy attack; again, the tower, by its very nature, is the least stable of all architectural structures and far more vulnerable to the effects of accident than other buildings.

The Romans built many lighthouses around the coasts of Europe; at least thirty are known to have existed and it is probable that there were many more. Not being a seafaring people themselves to any great extent they performed this service to encourage the great extension in trade which was a consequence of the peace they enforced in the western world. In his *Ecclesiastical History* Bede tells us that the Romans built many fortified towers for protection against the raids of Saxon and Danish pirates and that they were also used as lighthouses. He says that the old name for Whitby, Streonshalh, means *Sinus Fari*—Lighthouse Bay. The remains of a Roman light-tower can still be seen within Dover castle which ante-dates the second-century church of St Mary with which it is contiguous. It is an octagonal building of Roman workmanship consisting of green sandstone, Kentish rag and Roman brick. Each side is 14 feet wide and the lower parts of the walls are 10 feet thick. In 1259 it was encased in brick and a few years later an additional storey was added, bringing the total height to 40 feet. It was then used as a bell-tower for St Mary's church.

Although little is known about the origins of the Dover pharos there is much information on its opposite number which stood at Boulogne. It was originally built by Caligula as a monument to his renown but was adapted as a lighthouse in A.D. 191. From then until the collapse of the Roman Empire it guided Roman shipping between Dover and Boulogne. The tower was reconstructed by Charlemagne about A.D. 800 as a fortress and lighthouse combined and lasted another 800 years; but in 1645, as a result of the corroding action of the sea, the cliff supporting it collapsed, taking the old lighthouse with it.

Other remains of Roman light-towers still exist at Folkestone, Flamborough, St Andrews and in Wales, while at Burrow Wells, near Workington, on a hill near the sea stands a very ancient tower which still serves as a sea-mark. A few miles north of Whitby is Dunsley Bay village in the centre of which can be seen the ruins of an old tower which was certainly a sea-mark, if not a lighthouse, for early navigators. There are similar towers at the entrance to Milford Haven and to Morecambe Bay. The south end of Walney Island is known as Peel, from the ancient word 'pele' meaning tower, while the near-by headland bears the name of Furness, or Fire-ness.

The ancient geographer Strabo described a lighthouse at Caepio in Spain, which stood on a rock surrounded by sea. If this is true, then the claim of the first Eddystone lighthouse to be the original wave-swept tower is incorrect. A tall Roman lighthouse still stood at Corunna at the end of the eighteenth century. It was a square tower, built of small stones, and was 92 feet high. The means of access to the top was a curious and perilous one, consisting of a shallow channel cut into the outside of the masonry. One would have to crawl up and along this channel until a corner was reached and here it continued on the other side.

The Emperor Claudius built a fine light-tower at Ostia on the bank of the Tiber in A.D. 50. Modelled on the Pharos of Alexandria, it was 150 feet high. So dangerous were the waters there that a guild of divers existed to deal with the numerous wrecks at that point. Ostia lighthouse was said to rival the Pharos of Alexandria but this claim is a doubtful one, although it must be remembered that Ostia was then the chief port of Rome. Therefore its lighthouse must have been far more important than the one at Alexandria even if it did not rival it in size. As the power of Rome increased and imposed peace throughout the known world, so did the number of lighthouses and by the time of the decline of the Empire at least 30 lighthouses were in regular operation.

Towards the end of the fifth century the power of Rome retreated and was lost before the overwhelming tide of barbarism, and the withdrawal was followed by the collapse of civilized society. In the north of Britain the Picts and Scots swarmed over the Wall and into the vacuum left by the departed legions while the coasts of western Europe were savaged by pirates and raiders from the four points of the compass. The Roman love of building was replaced by vandalism, Roman culture by murder and massacre, Roman law by anarchy. The flow of international trade became a trickle, marine enterprise declined and shipbuilding became a lost art. The coastal lights of Europe and the Mediterranean changed from friendly warnings to invitations to become the victims of piracy and one by one they were extinguished. Europe was plunged into the gloom of the Dark Ages.

3

Philanthropists and Speculators

THE LIGHTHOUSE PLAYS no part in the history of the Dark Ages. The clock of progress having been turned back, the regularly maintained light atop a tower reverted to its primitive origin—a cautious glow from a bonfire or lantern exhibited at particular times for the guidance of particular vessels. Then, as the turmoil and lawlessness in Europe diminished, trade between nations gradually revived and the lights slowly returned. The Christianity introduced in Roman times survived the centuries of darkness and it was the monks, priests and hermits who began again the task of establishing and maintaining regular beacons.

In the corner of the tower of St Michael's Mount are the remains of a stone lantern known as St Michael's Chair, which was displayed by the monks for the guidance of local fishermen;[1] while Lantern Hill, near Ilfracombe, gets its name from an ancient chapel dedicated to St Nicholas where a fire was lit and maintained all night for the benefit of passing ships. In 1323 a chapel was privately built and endowed at St Catherine's, Isle of Wight, with the condition that the priest said daily masses for the family of the donor and maintained a nightly warning light for shipping. In the early fifteenth century a wealthy man turned hermit lived in a stone tower on a bank of the river Humber. He put a beacon on top of his tower, then asked and received the leave of King Richard II to levy a toll on all ships using the harbour, the proceeds to be spent on building a tall lighthouse and the maintenance of the light. The tower functioned for nearly two hundred years before the incoming sea destroyed both it and the

[1] According to the nineteenth-century antiquarian, Timbs, it was an old belief that any married woman who had the courage to climb the tower and sit in 'St Michael's Chair' would obtain the mastery of her husband.

hermitage. Although the coast in the area is particularly dangerous, this light was not replaced until the end of the seventeenth century.

East of the Needles, at about 300 feet above sea-level, are the ruins of an ancient chapel built by Walter de Godyton in 1323. Nine years before, de Godyton had brought some wine looted from a wrecked ship containing a cargo from the vineyards of the monks of Picardy, and he built the chapel as a self-imposed penance, endowing it with lands to provide for the living of a priest, one of whose duties was to show a light to warn of the dangers of St Catherine's Point.

The dissolution of the monasteries was a serious setback to English coastal lights for it swept away many of the men who had devoted their lives to the safety of seafarers, but their excellent example of disinterested humanitarianism had by then inspired many philanthropic laymen to build permanent towers with endowments as a means of maintaining the lights. By the end of the sixteenth century port and harbour authorities, with the less altruistic motive of protecting their trade, had joined the good work of the philanthropists and a regularly maintained system of lights was re-established around Europe.

In 1536, King Henry VIII, possibly becoming aware of one of the unfortunate side-effects of his persecution of the monks, granted a charter to the Guild of the Blessed Trinity at Newcastle which required it to

... found, build, make and frame of stone, lime and sand, by the best ways and means which they know or can, two towers, one, to wit, in the northern part of the Shelys [Shields] at the entrance of the port of the said town, and the other upon a hill there fit and convenient for signals, meets and bounds, for the safe and secure custody of the town and port aforesaid, and also of our subjects and others, being in our alliance, coming to the said town or port.

The Guild was empowered to impose tolls on passing ships, the proceeds of which were to maintain the towers and to keep 'a perpetual light' nightly on each. It functioned for over two hundred years.

In 1550 a European traveller in the Bosphorus observed a lighthouse that was very much before its time, and it is a pity that no other details concerning it have survived. It is described as an octagonal tower, 120 steps high, with leaded glass windows. On top was a great glass lantern, 12 feet in diameter and 9 feet high, lit by a copper pan of oil containing twenty floating wicks.

Although concerned with sea-marks rather than lights, the Act of Queen Elizabeth passed in 1565 demonstrates the increasing importance being attached to navigational aids in the sixteenth century. The Act made it an offence (punishable by a fine of £100 with the alternative of outlawry) to remove or alter any sea-mark.

Forsomuch as by destroying and taking away of certain steeples, woods and other marks standing upon the main shores adjoining to the sea coasts of this realm of England and Wales being as beacons and marks of ancient time accustomed for seafaring men . . . divers ships have by the lack of such marks of late years been miscarried, perished and lost in the sea.

It is certain that a sea-light was displayed at Genoa as early as 1160 for there are records of light dues being paid by shipping in that year. The present tower, which still serves as a sea-mark for coastal shipping, was built in 1544 to replace an earlier lighthouse that was at one time in the charge of Antonio Columbus, uncle to Christopher. The tower is 200 feet high, consisting of two shafts, one upon the other, of 30 feet and 23 feet square. Because of its height the Lanterna of Genoa was vulnerable to lightning. To counteract this a statue of St Christopher was placed on its summit; then, in 1778, a lightning conductor was installed.

Among the many others erected during the Middle Ages there were lighthouses at Dieppe, La Rochelle, Meloria, Leghorn and the Messina Straits, but permanent towers at this time were the exception. Most coastal lights were wood or coal fires burning in iron braziers, and apart from being very expensive to maintain (some of them burnt a ton of coal each night) they were not very efficient. When the wind blew off the land the sea side of the fire burnt brightly enough, but with a gale making a lee shore—and this was precisely the time when a light was essential for shipping—the sea side of the fire would be almost black. One of these open fires existed on the Isle of May, in the Firth of Forth, as late as 1816. It was a high tower, built in 1636, bearing a brazier which was tended by three men. Coal was raised by a simple pulley.

The estuary of the Gironde river empties into the Bay of Biscay and it is through this estuary that ships have sailed for centuries, trading in the famous wines of Bordeaux. Where the estuary meets the full force of the gales and currents of the Atlantic there is a group of rocks and shoals which were a fearful hazard to sailing ships. How many ships foundered or were smashed to pieces on these rocks and how many lives lost can never be known, but the wreckings became so numerous by the middle of the eleventh century that shipmasters refused to attempt the passage of the Gironde unless a light was set up to guide them. The alternative for the burghers and citizens of Bordeaux was a loss of a substantial portion of their trade. Consequently, within a short time of this demand, a wood-fired brazier was erected on that part of the reef known as Cordouan Rock. Four men were engaged to tend the fire and, to cover the cost of fuel and wages, a tax, graduated according to tonnage, was imposed on every vessel leaving or arriving at the port. This is the first example of the system of lighthouse dues which survives in England to this day. The fire served its purpose for nearly three hundred years, but when Edward the Black

Prince became the ruler of Gascony he built a tower some 40 feet high topped by a platform upon which a hermit maintained a fire at night. In 1581, the tower being in urgent need of repairs, King Henry III sent the architect Louis de Foix to Cordouan to estimate the cost of the work. De Foix was an experienced engineer as well as an architect; he had built bridges, docks and harbours in addition to public buildings and military works. He was also a skilled clockmaker.

His estimate for repairing the Cordouan lighthouse was so high, however, that the king decided instead to replace the old tower with a new one. De Foix was commissioned to design and build the new Cordouan light and the result was the most magnificent building in the history of pharology. De Foix's idea was to combine a beacon, church, royal residence and fortress in one building.

The Cordouan Rock was completely submerged at high tide and even at low water was difficult of access, the only landing place being a small beach of shingle where, in favourable weather, a small boat could be run up. Nevertheless, de Foix constructed on the rock a massive circular foundation, 135 feet in diameter and 8 feet high, which was solid apart from a square cavity in its centre which was to serve as a cellar. Rising from this platform, which was richly embellished, was a series of four cylindrical storeys of diminishing size. The ground floor, surrounded by an elegant balcony 50 feet in diameter, contained the living accommodation for four light-keepers. This was arranged around the wall while in the centre was a sumptuous entrance hall, 22 feet square by 20 feet high. From this a staircase led to the king's apartments on the first floor, consisting of an elegant *salon* with decorated pillars and murals, an ante-room and a number of closets. On the second floor was a domed chapel notable for its mosaic and, above this, a secondary lantern-room. The main lantern-room was at the top. Access between the upper storeys was provided by a spiral staircase. The whole of the interior, including the working-rooms, was elaborately decorated with carvings, sculptures, gilt work, pillars and arches. The style of the interior decorations anticipated the unfortunate taste for eclecticism that lay three hundred years ahead, for it is said that the pillars of the lowest storey were Doric, those of the next, Ionic, of the third, Corinthian, while those of the fourth a mixture of all three. The Tour de Cordouan took twenty-seven years to complete and it still ranks as the finest lighthouse ever built. In 1788 the upper part of the building was demolished and rebuilt in a more functional style and in this form it serves as a lighthouse today.

As we have seen, the first lights were established and maintained by philanthropists and it became the custom for these men to apply for a patent to exact dues from passing ships to cover the cost of fuel and labour. As the volume of shipping increased, the income from private lights became considerable and, inevitably, philanthropy gave way to speculation. The ownership of a light on a busy shipping lane could secure a huge income and these incomes often built up into vast family fortunes. When, in 1836, Trinity House was empowered to take over control of all English lights they had to pay £170,000 in compensation to one John Phillips, who owned and maintained a primitive wooden beacon on the Smalls. The Brethren of Trinity House had themselves obtained the original patent for this light and had sub-let it to the Phillips family on a ninety-nine year lease at £5 per annum. The member of the family with whom they originally dealt was a Liverpool Quaker and businessman who described his work in putting up the beacon as 'a great and holy good to serve and save humanity'. Nevertheless he served not only humanity, for by the end of the seventeenth century the income from his light had reached £11,000 per annum, making the repurchasing price quite a modest one.

Another proprietor who ran a small light on a barren rock demanded £550,000 from the Brethren to relinquish it and on being refused he took the case to arbitration where a jury awarded him £445,000—a sum which must represent about £4 million today. Thus, lighthouse-keeping became big business and a subject of political jobbery as influence was required to obtain these very lucrative patents. There is a note in the diary of Lord Grenville reminding him to watch for a good humour in the king that he might 'ask him for a lighthouse', while in 1661 Samuel Pepys was offered one-eighth of the profits if he would support the application for a lighthouse patent made by one Captain Murford.

A very fine example of an old privately-owned coal-fire tower can still be seen, though now no longer used as a lighthouse, on St Agnes Island in the Scillies. Even the iron brazier is still in existence; it is now in use as an ornamental flower bowl.

Because of the immense cost of fuel some private patentees were tempted to keep their fires down to a minimum, but generally they built good strong towers and maintained bright lights. Apart from the initial cost of establishing the light and the cost of fuel the old private owner had few other outgoings. The wages he paid to his light-keeper were trifling. In 1628 a man named Hill was engaged as keeper of Caistor light at a salary of £37 per annum. In turn he appointed an old woman to carry out his duties at a much lower wage. Unfortunately she lived many miles away from the beacon and in bad weather, when the light was most needed, she stayed at home leaving the light unlit. This state of affairs lasted for over thirty years and it was not until a ship was lost through the failure of the Caistor light that Hill was dismissed.

In 1619 a Cornishman, Sir John Killegrew, applied to King James I for a charter to erect a beacon on the Lizard Point. He also asked the king for a grant of twenty nobles a year for the upkeep of the light and for permission to ask for *voluntary* contributions from passing ships. The king passed Killegrew's petition to Trinity House for their opinion and the Brethren replied that not only was a light on Lizard Point unnecessary, it would be an invitation to pirates or enemies. Nevertheless, the petition was granted with the proviso that the light should be extinguished at times when the approach of hostile ships was likely. Killegrew soon discovered that Trinity House was not the only source of opposition to his plan; finding great difficulty in obtaining local labour and materials to build his lighthouse he made the bitter complaint that the work

. . . has been more chargeable and troublesome than I expected for the inhabitants near think they suffer in this erection. They affirm I take away God's grace from them. Their English meaning is that now they shall receive no more benefit by shipwreck, for this will prevent it. They have been so long used to reap profit by the calamities of the ruin of shipping, that they claim it to be hereditary, and hourly complain to me but I hope they will now husband their land, which their former idle life has omitted in the assurance of their gain by shipwreck.

However, in spite of the opposition, Killegrew built his tower and exhibited a light from it on Christmas Day, 1619. In the spring of the following year he reported to the Lord High Admiral of England that a ship had been wrecked near the Lizard, 'through not having notice that any such light was there maintained and the men drunk, it being confessed by them that are saved'. Complaining that the lighthouse had cost him £500 and he had received as yet no return, Killegrew went on to ask 'whether I shall continue the light or not for the charge lies so heavy'. Eventually he obtained the right to levy a due of ½d per ton on passing ships and his lighthouse showed a profit of £400 a year.

With the imposition of the dues, opposition to the light spread from the wrecking community to their potential victims, the shipmasters; they objected to paying for a beacon which, they asserted, could not be seen during murky weather and which was quite unnecessary when visibility was good. The opponents to the Lizard light also raised the old objection that it would be an invitation to pirates to raid the coast (to be answered by Sir William Monson that 'the pirates coming from our coast is not so much to rob and spoil as to be provided with victuals and necessaries and to make sale of their stolen goods'). Eventually, in the face of so much hostility and lacking sufficient money to maintain it, Killegrew was forced to extinguish his light. The Lizard was left in the dark for the next one hundred years.

Sir John Killegrew's abortive attempt to light one of the most perilous points on the English coast had left him £600 out of pocket but he appears to have been a resourceful man for in 1627 he was found leading a gang of wreckers who, having threatened the crew with death, were busy plunder-

ing the cargo of a grounded ship. Recalling the words of those Cornish-
men against whom he had so recently railed, Sir John claimed wrecker's
rights 'through custom and descent'.

4

Winstanley's Tower on Eddystone Rock

FOURTEEN MILES OFF Plymouth lie three reefs of the rare red rock, granitoid gniess. At high water they are almost submerged, and even on the calmest of days the water eddies wickedly and continuously around the middle rock which is known as Eddystone. For centuries these rocks took a regular toll of ships passing through the English Channel; so notorious were they that mariners tended to give them the widest possible berth—so wide sometimes that in taking a course to the southward many a captain found himself in dire trouble amongst the rocks that litter the French coast and the Channel Islands. When the brigantine *Mayflower*, with the Pilgrim Fathers aboard, sailed out from Plymouth on 6 September 1620, on its hazardous three-month crossing of the North Atlantic, her captain noted in his log

a wicked reef of twenty-three rust-red rocks lying nine and one half miles south of Rame Head on the Devon mainland, great ragged stones around which the sea constantly eddies, a great danger to all ships hereabouts, for they sit astride the entrance to this harbour and are exposed to the full force of the westerly winds and must always be dreaded by mariners. Leaving Plymouth, we managed to avoid this reef but ships making harbour must stand well to the south and this is difficult in stormy weather, for if any vessel makes too far to the south as likely as not she will be caught in the prevailing strong current and swept to her doom on those evil rocks.

World trade expanded considerably during the course of the seventeenth century; consequently ships, crews and cargoes grew bigger as ports increased in size. The city of Plymouth took a good share in the increased prosperity and so it followed that Eddystone Rock claimed *its* share.

In a patent roll signed by William and Mary in 1694 the 'Master Wardens and Assistants of the Trinity House' were empowered to 'erect a Lighthouse or Beacon with a light upon a rock called the Eddystone off Plymouth' and to exact a due from all ships passing the lighthouse of 'one penny per tunn outward bound and alsoe one penny per tunn inward excepting Coasters [who were to pay] twelve pence for each Voyage passing by the said Lighthouse or Beacon and noe more'. No ship was to be permitted to unload or receive service until the dues were paid.

Armed with this document the Brethren came to an arrangement with a Plymouth citizen named Walter Whitfield, whereby he was to finance and build the lighthouse, receiving in return the whole of the light dues for five years. For the next fifty years the income would be equally shared between him and Trinity House after which time the lighthouse and the entire dues would revert to Trinity House.

The man who was to carry out the formidable task of building on the Eddystone was one of many parts. Born in 1644, Henry Winstanley was an accomplished engraver, painter, inventor and designer. He was also an inveterate practical joker who filled his house with elaborate devices of his own invention which must have guaranteed his family a laugh a minute when visitors arrived. There were chairs that imprisoned the sitter and others that slowly rose into the air. There were doorways that were not doorways at all but optical illusions effected with mirrors, which were liable to damage the noses of persons trying to pass through them. There were various objects lying on the floor which, when picked up or kicked aside, caused frightening apparitions to appear. One caller at the house described his experiences:

We visited the famous Mr Winstanley's ingenious contrivances, viz., at the taking up of a slipper there appeared the form of a ghost which arose from the planching [floor], and disappeared again. A small pair of organs played a tune at your winding up. One chair my cousin Tresillian sat in it descended perpendicularly about ten feet in a dark and dismal place. Another chair he sat in it ran the length of a small orchard and over a moat, jumped up in a tree, then descended and in a very little time stopped. A seat in the garden was changed into several shapes.

In 1695 Winstanley was fifty-one, a very wealthy man and the owner of five ships; by the end of that year he only owned three for the other two had been claimed by the dreaded Eddystone Rock. On the news of the second loss, Winstanley travelled to Plymouth and demanded of the authorities there that something be done about lighting Eddystone. He was told that the lighthouse would be built when Whitfield and his associates could find an architect to design it but that up to then they had had no success. A man of Winstanley's temperament could not see where the difficulty lay. Seeking out Walter Whitfield, he undertook to design and build a tower on Eddystone himself. His proposal was accepted.

For the site of his lighthouse Winstanley had little or no choice for there was only one rock on the reef that was not submerged at high tide. The shape and situation of this rock was daunting. On one side it rose almost vertically out of the sea and on the other it sloped down sharply at an angle of thirty degrees. During ideal summer weather it was theoretically possible to work on the rock for three hours a day while the journey between Plymouth and the site took up to six hours each way. Winstanley, who it must be remembered was fifty-one years old, made many trips himself and, explaining why the work took three years to complete, he wrote that it was

not for the greatness of the work but for the difficulty and danger of getting backward and forward to that place, nothing being or could be left there for the first two years but what was most throughly affixed to the rock or the work at very extraordinary charge. And though nothing could be attempted to be done but in the summer season, yet the weather then at times would prove so bad that for ten or fourteen days together the sea would be so raging about these rocks— caused by outwinds and the running of the ground seas coming from the main ocean—that though the weather should seem to be most calm in other places, yet here it would mount and fly more than two hundred foot as has been so found since there was a lodgement upon the place. And therefore all our works were constantly buried at those times and exposed to the mercy of the seas and no power was able to come near to make good or help anything, as I have often experienced with my workmen in a boat in great danger: only having the satisfaction to see my work imperfectly at times as the seas fell from it at a mile or two distance—and this at the prime of the year and no wind or appearance of bad weather.

Winstanley made his first landing on the rock in June 1696 and his first task was to bore twelve holes to take the stout iron stanchions that were to anchor the lighthouse to the reef. Strong and skilful though his men were, it took them nearly five months to sink those twelve holes. The rock was so hard that the picks made little impression on it. In bad weather, after a harrowing journey of six hours, the men were already exhausted by the time they landed. The holes were finally completed at the end of October and there was just time enough to secure the stanchions with molten lead before winter brought an end to the first season.

Winstanley's tower (Plate 1a) looked extraordinary to say the least. It has been described as being more suitable for a Chinese cemetery than for the English Channel. Had the sea been sentient it would have chuckled grimly as the richly embellished wooden structure rose slowly from its stone base. It must be remembered, however, that Winstanley's lighthouse was the first to be built on an isolated wave-swept rock and this particular rock was exposed to the full force and fury of the Atlantic Ocean. Hydrography and hydrokinetics were unknown sciences in those days and there was no means of measuring the destructive forces of the wind. But puny and inadequate though Winstanley's effort might now appear, it was a valiant one, the eventual failure of which supplied the theoretical basis for the development of the art and science that eventually produced the subtle masterpiece of pharology, the parabolic tower, many examples of which have resisted the persistent powers of the sea for over a century and a half.

The summer of 1697 was devoted to the construction of the solid 12-foot stone base upon which the wooden tower was to be built. Local granite was used—cut and dressed in Plymouth to suit the slope of the rock. As England was at war with France the working party was provided by the Admiralty with H.M.S. *Terrible* to protect them, but on a late day in June when the warship did not show up, a lurking French privateer sent a boat to the rock to take Winstanley to France as a prisoner. Louis XIV, hearing of the incident, punished the privateer, loaded Winstanley with presents and returned him to England with the message: 'I am at war with England, not with humanity.' By the end of the season the Herculean task of unshipping the heavy blocks of granite and building the solid section of the base was complete. There was now a level platform well above the reach of the waves upon which a hoisting tackle could be erected for the next stage of the work. During the following winter Winstanley had second thoughts about the base of the tower and the next season was spent in increasing its diameter to 16 feet and its height to 18 feet.

In 1698 the hollow section of the tower was constructed, making it possible for the men to live within it, thus eliminating the time-wasting voyage to and from work. But on the first night spent on the rock a fierce storm blew up. Winstanley described that hectic night:

We ventured to lodge there soon after midsummer for greater dispatch of this work, but the first night the weather came bad and so continued, that it was eleven days before any boat could come near us again, and not being acquainted with the height of the seas rising, we were nearly all the time near drowned with wet and all our provisions in as bad a condition, though we worked night and day as much as possible to make shelter for ourselves. In this storm we lost some of our materials although we did what we could to save them. But the boat then returning we all left the house to be refreshed on shore, and as soon as the weather did permit, we returned again.

Working in the shelter of the tower's stone base, Winstanley and his men soon completed the wooden superstructure and on 14 November

1698 the tallow candles which were the lantern's illuminant were lit by Winstanley himself. The first yellow glow which was to check Eddystone's insatiable appetite for ships and lives was the cause of great celebrations in and around Plymouth. A few persons were unable to join the revels for, wrote Winstanley, 'we put up the light on the 14th of November 1698. Which being so late in the year it was three days before Christmas before we had a relief to get ashore again, and were almost at the last extremity for want of provisions, but by good providence then two boats came with provisions and the family that was to take care of the light, and so ended this year's work.'

The following winter was a severe one, but it was the first for centuries in which no ships were lost on Eddystone Rock. In the spring, Winstanley visited his lighthouse and carried out a detailed inspection; the results of this were disturbing, for the constant action of the spray had prevented the cement from properly setting and the pointing of the stonework was in a very bad condition. In addition, Winstanley learned from the keepers that the structure had trembled and shuddered under the pounding of the waves. It was obvious that the tower would not survive another winter like the last unless it was strengthened considerably. During the summer, Winstanley again increased the girth and height of the stone pillar, making it 24 feet in diameter and 20 feet high. The joints were repointed and, to protect them, they were covered with bands of iron. The wooden section was strengthened and heightened by 25 feet making the overall height of the building 120 feet. The work was finished by the end of the season and then Winstanley occupied himself in executing and publishing a drawing of the building with an explanatory text. The crane he describes as 'an engine crane that parts at joints to be taken off when not in use, the rest being fastened to the side of the house to save it in time of storms, and it is to be made use of to help landing on the rock, which without is very difficult'. The gallery above the crane was 'to take in goods and provisions from the boat to the storeroom'. The window to the left of the gallery is 'of a very fine bedchamber with a chimney and a closet, the room being richly gilded and painted and the outside shutters very strongly barred'. The next floor was given over to 'the State Room, being 10 square [sic], 19 foot wide, and 12 foot high, very well carved and painted, with a chimney and 2 closets, and 2 sash windows with strong shutters to bar and bolt'. Over the State Room was 'the Airry or open Gallery where is conveniency to crane up goods and a great leaden cistern to hold the rainwater that falls from upper roofs in pipes and to let the sea pass through in times of storms'. The semi-domed room within the gallery was the kitchen which contained 'a large chimney, oven, dressers, and table, with a large closet and a large standing bed'. Above this room was 'a bedchamber with 2 cabin beds and all conveniences for a dining room with large lockers to hold a great store of candles for lights'. The lantern itself is described as 'the lanthorn that holds the lights is 8 square [*sic*], 11 foot diameter, 15 foot high in the upright wall: having 8 great glass windows, and ground plates for squares, and conveniency to burn 60 candles at a time besides the great hanging lamp. There is a door to go into the gallery that is all round, to cleanse the glass of the lanthorn, which is often dimmed by salt water that washes it in storms.' On a level with the 'semi-dome' can be seen 'a gallery to go out to put [*sic*] the ensign or make a signal' while from this gallery is suspended 'a vessel to lay float on the water to take in small things from a boat on the west side of the rock when there is no landing on the other side'. The crane on the right of the gallery was 'a large standing crane to take things at a distance when no boats can come near the rock'. The large candlesticks outside the lantern were, of course, purely decorative although Winstanley gives a practical use for them: 'the irons that bears them are very useful to stay a ladder to clear the glass'. The cylindrical object on the right of the lantern gallery is 'a moving engine trough to cast down stones to defend the landing place in case of need'.

The enlarged and improved lighthouse guarded its rock for another four years during which time Eddystone claimed no victims. Then, on 26 November 1703, Winstanley landed on the reef with a party of workmen to carry out some urgent repairs. That same night there occurred the most cataclysmic storm ever to be recorded in England's West Country. Roofs, trees, church spires—even whole buildings—were smashed to the ground in the horror of that storm. It was recorded that eight hundred dwelling houses alone were completely destroyed, together with four hundred windmills. At least 123 people were killed on land and it was feared that no fewer than eight thousand sailors died in 150 shipwrecks. That night the lantern on Eddystone showed its light at the usual time and it was observed from the shore until the walls of rain reduced the visibility to a few yards. When daylight came the Eddystone Rock was seen to have regained its aeons-old appearance. The lighthouse had vanished and with it the noble Winstanley, his men and the family of keepers.

That curious and intriguing character Henry Winstanley once boasted that it was his greatest wish to be in his tower 'during the greatest storm that ever was seen'. He got his wish.

Two nights after the ocean annihilated Winstanley and his work, the merchantman *Winchelsea*, homeward bound from America, sailed into the Channel. Having, by a near miracle, weathered the great storm, the crew considered themselves home and dry as they peered into the darkness for the Eddystone light. The first indication they received of the near vicinity of the dreaded reef was the sound and sight of roaring white water—and by then it was far too late. With a horrible shudder the *Winchelsea* scraped over the rocky teeth of the reef and within minutes she split against the rocks to founder with all but two of her people. The Eddystone Rock was whetting its appetite.

5

Rudyerd and Smeaton on Eddystone

NOTHING FURTHER SEEMS to have been done about Eddystone until a year after the fall of Winstanley's tower. Then, at the beginning of 1705, Trinity House gave permission to Captain John Lovet to build a lighthouse on the reef through the grant of a ninety-nine year lease at £100 per annum. Whitfield, having relinquished his lease with over forty years of it unexpired, must have had enough of the Eddystone Rock, for he and his co-entrepreneurs were considerably out of pocket. Winstanley himself had got back only £2,000 of the £5,000 he had put into the enterprise.

The design of the second lighthouse was again put into the hands of an amateur architect, possibly because the professionals fought shy of the task, and it was a wealthy silk mercer, John Rudyerd, who undertook the replacement of Winstanley's effort. In those days science and invention were largely in the hands of wealthy gentlemen and, in this case, Lovet's choice of a designer was a good one. After carefully studying the drawings and a model of Winstanley's tower, Rudyerd concluded that its very mass had contributed to its fall. He then calculated that as a massive stone tower had been unable to withstand the forces of wind and sea to which Eddystone Rock was subject, only timber would possess the necessary resilience to survive such a storm as had occurred in 1703. He designed a tapering tower of wood—slim and circular—within which were alternating courses of timber and granite and a stout timber mast running through the centre from top to bottom (see Plate 1b). In Smeaton's later words

[Rudyerd] saw the errors in the former building and avoided them. Instead of a polygon he chose a circle for the outline of his building and carried up the elevation in that form. He seems to have adopted ideas . . . the very reverse of his predecessor, for all the unwieldy ornaments at the top, the open gallery, the projecting cranes, and other contrivances more for ornament and pleasure than for use, Mr Rudyerd laid totally aside.

In his application of the principles of aerodynamics to the design of an exposed tower, Rudyerd established himself as the father of modern light-house building. After experiencing all the delays and frustrations that are still associated with landing on Eddystone, Rudyerd began building operations in the spring of 1706. Having appreciated the mistake of build-ing on a slope, his first concern was to cut the slope into a series of steps but even this comparatively simple work was beyond the power of the primitive tools of the time. When attacked with hammer and chisel the rock chipped off in uneven flakes, and rather than a series of horizontal surfaces Rudyerd had to be satisfied with somewhat rough-shaped steps. As against Winstanley's twelve, Rudyerd drove thirty-six holes into the rock to take the anchoring irons, and to ensure a perfectly dry joint a most ingenious method was used to fix them. Water was completely removed from each hole with a sponge, the hole then being immediately filled with molten tallow that was allowed to set. The iron to be fixed was then heated and plunged into the hole causing the tallow to melt and over-flow; molten lead was then poured into the remaining space between iron and hole, forcing out the rest of the tallow and leaving a perfectly tight and dry joint between rock and iron. On this substantial anchorage was built the solid base of the tower consisting of oak baulks, firmly fitted and tied together with trenails and screw bolts, alternating with courses of Cornish moorstone jointed and cramped with iron. The solid base was continued for 9 feet above the highest point of the rock then further continued as a semi-solid tower containing a central shaft for the stairs. The semi-solid construction was carried on to a height of 36 feet and was then encased by shipwrights in seventy-one upright timbers which continued a further 34 feet above the wood and stone construction and formed the wooden wall of the living-quarters, store-rooms and lantern-room. Finally the seams of the outer skin were caulked and pitched like the hull of a ship. 'The whole building,' wrote Smeaton, 'consisted of a simple figure, being an elegant frustrum of a cone, unbroken by any projecting ornament, or anything whereon the violence of the storms could lay hold.'

The light, consisting of twenty-four tallow candles weighing 2 lb. each, was exhibited from the completed tower in the autumn of 1709.

Rudyerd's lighthouse carried out its purpose for forty-six years, its massive yet resilient construction defying the worst of Atlantic winters; but like the wooden ships upon which it was modelled it was vulnerable to the most dreaded of maritime disasters. On the night of 1 December 1755 the wooden lantern-room took fire from the guttering candles. The blaze travelled swiftly downwards enveloping the wooden floors one by one until the whole tower was a blazing beacon. No reef before or since was ever so adequately lit. For the three keepers, unable to be rescued because of the heavy sea, it was terrifying. In the confined space of the rock there was nowhere to hide from the shower of molten lead, red-hot bolts and blazing timbers that fell from the pillar of fire. One of the keepers, a man of ninety-four years, named Henry Hall, staring upward open-mouthed at the burning cupola, suddenly screamed to his companions that some molten lead had gone down his throat. The old man's companions were far too concerned in dodging the flaming debris to take much notice of him and anyway he seemed none the worse. All night long the three men crouched on the wave-swept rock scorched by the heat of the fire on one side, frozen by the icy wind and sea on the other, hardly able to evade the falling fragments because of the slippery stone. Thus they remained for eight hours until a fishing boat was able to put out from near-by Cawsend. A rope was thrown and one by one the unfortunate men, half dead from fear and exposure, were dragged through the fierce freezing water and hauled aboard the tossing boat. The first man across was Henry Hall, still loudly complaining that he had swallowed a mouthful of molten lead but as he showed no symptoms of such a mishap he was not believed.

By noon on the 2nd the tower was still burning and a sloop sent by the Navy arrived on the scene to attempt to save what remained of the solid base. But the swelling sea made it impossible for them to land the fire engine that they had brought out. The sailors could do nothing but watch as the timber courses of the base burned out to release the granite blocks which, one by one, tumbled into the sea. All that remained in the afternoon were thirty-six heat-twisted iron stakes sticking up from the rock like giant corkscrews.

By the time he got ashore poor old Henry Hall was beginning to show the effects of his experience. He had been badly burned at the start of the fire, had spent eight hours clinging to the sea-swept rock in an icy wind and had been hauled through the sea to the rescuing boat. That a man of ninety-four had survived such an ordeal was almost unbelievable, and when he insisted to the doctor that he had swallowed some molten lead it was thought that he was raving. Six days after the fire, Hall sat up in bed and began eating solid food. This improvement continued for a week but on the twelfth day he collapsed and died. His doctor decided to perform a post-mortem and, upon opening the old man's stomach, he found an oval-shaped piece of lead weighing over 7 oz.[1]

In 1724 the lease of Eddystone Rock had passed into the hands of a Robert Weston and his two partners and it was fortunate that they were men who put their responsibility to humanity before their business interests. Of the original lease only forty-eight years remained to run and

[1] The lead can be seen today at the Royal Scottish Museum at Edinburgh.

Weston, who acted for his partners, could well have thought in terms of replacing Rudyerd's light with one that would merely see out the remains of the lease. Instead he was resolved to build, regardless of cost, a structure that would last. With this idea in mind he asked the Royal Society to recommend an engineer to build a new tower on Eddystone. The president of the Society, the Earl of Macclesfield, unhesitatingly named John Smeaton, and Weston at once approached him on the subject.

Smeaton, the son of a solicitor, was born near Leeds in 1724. From infancy he had shown the most remarkable powers of observation. Like most boys he had the ability to take his toys to pieces, but unlike most boys he was able to put them together again. When still a child he gained the ability to make working models of pumps and windmills from wood and scraps of metal, and he never tired of observing carpenters, masons and millwrights at work. He once took a particularly keen interest in the erection of a steam-engine at Garforth coal-mine, and once having grasped the principle of steam power he built a miniature steam-engine and pump of his own. To test its efficiency he set it up by the fishpond in his father's garden and succeeded in pumping the pond dry, causing the demise of his father's fish. It was intended that Smeaton should follow his father's profession, but at the age of eighteen he broke away from his legal studies and became apprenticed to an instrument-maker. At the time he was approached by Weston, Smeaton was thirty-one and already considerably experienced in a wide field of engineering that included the building of canals, docks and harbours. One of the only forms of marine architecture he had not tried was lighthouse building, but nevertheless he accepted the task of building Eddystone's third tower and set to work immediately to study the problems involved in building a sea-proof, wind-proof and fire-proof tower on one of the most inaccessible, desolate rocks in the world.

Smeaton's first conclusion was that the tower must be built of stone and that it must be of very great weight, the stones being fixed together in such a way that the finished building would resemble a monolith in strength. But how could this be done? There was no quick-drying cement in those days, and with the constant wash of sea and spray the cement might never properly dry out. This was a difficulty that Winstanley had encountered and it is likely that this was a contributary cause of the eventual failure of his tower. After rejecting various schemes for fixing the stones with iron cramps, the idea gradually grew in Smeaton's mind that the blocks of masonry could be *dovetailed* together. Perfect rigidity was obtained by dovetailing timber—so why not dovetail stone? Smeaton took his idea to the proprietors, then to the Admiralty and, finally, to Trinity House. They were accepted and Smeaton made his way to Plymouth to take his first look at the notorious Eddystone Rock.

The engineer had to wait seven days before weather conditions allowed

him to leave the land and even then the violence of the sea around the
rock made a landing impossible. 'I had a good view of the rock,' he wrote,
'and an early opportunity of correcting the many errors that I had been led
into by the incorrectness of the several models and draughts which had
come into my hands.' After waiting another three days, Smeaton at last
landed on the rock at the end of a journey that, like those made by Winstanley, took six hours. The first visit to Plymouth lasted two months and
during that time only ten trips could be made to the rock. However,
Smeaton learned enough during this time to return to London to prepare
detailed plans for his lighthouse. As soon as these designs were approved
he returned to Plymouth, stopping off at Dorchester on the way where he
ordered a supply of Portland stone in blocks weighing from one to two
tons apiece. Before engaging his work force, Smeaton, with his usual
thoroughness, drew up a 'Plan for carrying on the works and Management
of the Workmen'. It is worth reproducing in full:

1 That the Eddystone service should by all reasonable inducements be ren-
dered preferable to any other common employment.
2 That therefore (as a punishment) any one failing his duty should be immediately discharged.
3 That the workmen should be divided into two companies; one company to be
out at the rock, the other to be employed in the workyard on shore.
4 That every Saturday, the weather permitting, these two companies to change
places; but the out-company not to return home till the in-company is carried
out to relieve them.
5 Every man to have certain fixed wages weekly; and the same whether in or out.
6 Every man to receive something per hour over and above the fixed wages, for
every hour he works upon the rock.
7 Every out-man to take all opportunities of landing upon the rock to work,
when the weather serves, whether night or day, Sundays or work-days.
8 The in-company not to work either nights or on Sundays, except in case of
necessity . . .
9 All extra work on shore to be paid for in proportion to double the fixed wages
for the like time.
10 The seamen to be also at constant weekly wages, with an addition of a fee
certain and proportionable every tide's work upon the rock.
11 Each company to have a foreman constantly with them while working upon
the rock; to be paid more than the common workmen, and in the same proportion.
12 The engineer and his deputy to go off alternately week for week; and each
week to go off as often, and stay as long as weather will permit, or the service
require.
13 In case of sickness, or necessary absence of either the engineer or deputy, the
whole (if possible) to be taken care of by the other.
14 All persons to victual themselves, but a bowl of punch to be allowed each
company on their return ashore.

15 The foremen, workmen and seamen, to be paid every time the respective companies return on shore.

16 All work tools to be provided and repaired at the charge of the proprietors, and to have a mark put upon each of them peculiar to Eddystone.

17 Every person hurt or maimed in the out-service to receive his common wages while under the surgeon's hands; and the proprietors to pay the surgeon. This to be allowed on the certificate of the engineer, deputy or agent.

18 Any person desirous of quitting the service, to give a week's notice to the engineer or deputy.

19 The foreman on shore to take an account of everything received into or sent out of the workyard; as also of the day's works of the company with him; under the check of the engineer or his deputy when on shore.

20 All smith's and plumber's work to be seen weighed by the foreman, engineer, or deputy on shore; and all timber or wood work to be measured, and other materials taken account of by the same on receiving them.

21 The foreman afloat to take account of time and landings upon the rock, to be checked by the engineer or his deputy when afloat.

22 An account of all matters done on shore to be given in weekly to the agent or accountant; and of all things done afloat by the proper foreman at the time of landing.

One of Smeaton's 'reasonable inducements' was the high rate of pay he offered his men:

Grade	Rate per day away from shore	Rate per day on shore	Bonus per hour for time spent on the rock
Masons	2s 6d	1s 8d	9d
Miners	2s 0d	1s 6d	8d
Two Foremen (each)	5s 0d	3s 6d	1s 0d

Smeaton recruited his labour force in Plymouth and here also he hired workyards where the stones were to be dressed, vessels to transport men and materials, and the eighty-ton buss *Neptune* that was to be anchored off Eddystone as a floating store-house and dormitory for the men and as a temporary Eddystone light. Work on the rock began on 3 August 1756, every moment of fine weather being used. When possible a shift system continued the work throughout the night. On the other hand, sometimes men landing between spells of dirty weather could only work for as little as one hour before being forced back to the *Neptune*. By 22 November the cutting, dovetailing and boring of the rock foundation being finished, Smeaton and his party boarded the *Neptune* to return to Plymouth for the winter. There was, no doubt, a cheerful air among the out-gang as the *Neptune* pulled up her anchor and turned her bows toward Plymouth. They had had a hard and perilous summer season and now they looked forward to the six months of shore comfort that would start with the bowl of punch to which they were entitled on landing. Unfortunately that bowl of punch was still a long way off, for the gale that had been blowing throughout the day suddenly increased to a near-hurricane, driving the *Neptune* far off her course for Plymouth. Smeaton, resting below in the cabin, heard a sudden commotion on deck. 'It being very dark,' he wrote, 'the first thing I saw was the horrible appearance of the breakers almost surrounding us; John Bowden, one of the seamen, crying out "For God's sake, heave hard at the rope if you mean to save your lives". I immediately laid hold of a rope at which he himself was heaving as well as the other seamen, though he was also managing the helm. I not only hauled with all my strength but called to and encouraged the workmen to do the same thing.'

The ship was making directly for the rocks and in this situation her jib sail was blown to pieces and there was every possibility of the loss of the mainsail when the ship, answering her helm, came round. Not knowing his position, the captain wisely made for the open sea, and after a night during which the ship was constantly swept by waves he found it driving towards the Bay of Biscay. Again the ship was steered towards the Cornish coast and by evening it was within sight of Land's End. After two more storm-tossed nights the *Neptune* made Plymouth Sound.

Throughout the following winter Smeaton and his men were occupied ashore in preparing the stones for the next year's working. Each course was assembled with the one immediately above and below it then put aside to await the spring.

On 12 June 1757 the first stone, weighing 2½ tons, was landed on the rock and fixed in position. One by one the other stones, each numbered and lettered to identify its position, were hoisted onto the rock with a pair of sheerlegs and dovetailed to their neighbours. Not only were the stones dovetailed together but each was also locked to its neighbour by trenails. Additional strength was provided by binding the courses together vertically with one-foot-square marble plugs. By the end of October, nine courses had been laid without serious accident and the work party returned to shore to prepare the stones for the third season.

Work on the rock started again in May 1758 and, on landing, Smeaton had the satisfaction of seeing that his work remained intact in spite of a stormy winter. By the end of the year the twenty-fourth course had been reached and the building was 35 feet above the rock. Because of a particularly bitter winter it was not possible to start the fourth season until 5 July 1759, but as the top of the building was now well out of the sea's reach the work advanced rapidly. By 17 August 46 courses had been laid and the 70-foot-high tower was complete. The last of the masonry work was the cutting of the words 'Laus Deo' over the door of the lantern-room. The ironwork of the balcony and the lantern were next erected and the gilt ball on top of the cupola was screwed into place by Smeaton himself who performed this dizzy task while standing on four boards nailed together resting on the cupola which Roger Cornthwaite, his assistant, balanced by standing on the other end. Even then Smeaton's work was not complete, for as labour could not be obtained to finish the window fittings, the engineer did this himself. The chandelier of twenty-two candles was first lit on 16 October 1759 and Smeaton's lighthouse continued to light the Eddystone Rock for 140 years. As a testimony to the stability of the tower, Samuel Smiles quotes from a letter he received in 1848 when the tower was eighty-nine years old:

Mr Walker, the Harbour Master of Plymouth, has to make an annual inspection of the Eddystone Lighthouse. Not long ago, it struck him as a thing to be ascertained, whether the building was exactly perpendicular. For this purpose he let fall a plummet and found that the building was a *quarter-of-an-inch* off the perpendicular towards the North-east side. This he thought an alarming thing, as it might be the symptom of a settlement taking place in the foundation . . . but happening to look into a 'Life of Smeaton' . . . he found a record in his diary or journal to this effect: 'This day, the Eddystone Lighthouse has, thank God, been completed. It is, I believe, perfect; except that it inclines a quarter-of-an-inch from the perpendicular towards the North-east'. Thus, in the long lapse of time since it was built, it stands precisely as it stood at the moment of its completion.

Smeaton's tower took over three years to build and yet the actual time spent on the rock totalled less than sixteen weeks. During that short space of time 1,493 blocks of granite had been interlocked and secured with 700 marble plugs, 1,800 trenails and 4,500 wedges.[1] It was a prodigious feat of engineering, marking a new era in lighthouse building that stretches through the nineteenth century down to the present day. 'In justice to him,' wrote James Watt, 'we should observe that he lived before Rennie, and before there were one-tenth of the artists there are now. His example and precepts have made us all engineers.'

[1] The fame of Smeaton's lighthouse was perpetuated by the English penny upon which coin it appeared periodically from 1860 until 1970.

6

The Last of the Amateurs

ALTHOUGH THE ACTIVITIES of Rudyerd and Smeaton were to revolutionize the practice of lighthouse building it was to be some time before their ideas were generally adopted. Throughout most of the eighteenth century the open fire was still very much the rule although the number of sea-lights slowly increased all over the world. Even the Chinese set up a light on the south-west extremity of Fisher Island, off Formosa; this was an oil-burning lantern made of oyster shells, built by public subscription and maintained by a light due imposed on every junk entering Ma Kung harbour. Its range was said to be about a mile. Other lights were established in Japan, India, on the Nile Delta and the Bosphorus and in Havana, while in 1740 the French erected the first Canadian lighthouse at their fortress of Louisburg on Cape Breton Island, Nova Scotia. Eighteen years later a tower was built on Sambro Island near the entrance to Halifax harbour and its replacement erected 148 years later is still in operation.

The first American lighthouse was erected in Boston in 1716 but the whole North American coast was very badly lit until, in 1789, the Federal Government of the United States set up a Lighthouse Establishment. The full history of the lights of the United States is dealt with in later chapters.

The success of Smeaton's tower on Eddystone reef caused a widespread demand for lights on isolated rocks which had hitherto been regarded as impossible to build upon—a demand both from seamen and port authorities on one side and speculators on the other. In 1658 there had been a concerted demand from some shipowners to light the dangerous group of rocks off Anglesey, known as the Skerries, but because of the apparent inaccessibility nothing was done. After Rudyerd things were different. If a tower could be built on Eddystone, one could be built anywhere in the world, and it was this thought that inspired one, William Trench, to ask for and obtain a ninety-nine-year lease to build a lighthouse on the Skerries at a first year's rent of £10 and £20 per annum thereafter.

In 1714 he sent his son with six men and some materials to the rock to start the preparations, but their small boat capsized and all were drowned. By 1717 Trench, for an outlay of £3,000, had managed to erect a tower '150 feet higher than the sea around it' and started to collect light dues at the rate of 1d per ton. Either because he was unable to collect all his dues, or for some other reason, the lighthouse did not pay and Trench, burdened by his capital costs and the outlay of £100 per year for maintaining the light, spent the rest of his life in debt. On his death in 1729 Trench's family, on account of his loss, obtained an Act of Parliament that vested the lighthouse in them 'for ever'.

A typical light bill of the time which accounted for Skerries dues, among others, reads as follows:

Coast   Number 7256
PORT OF LIVERPOOL

Received the 12th day of May 1767 of John Hubbard, Master of the "William", a British Vessel, Burthen one hundred and thirty tons, arrived from Lynn, and now bound to London, the sum of ten shillings and ten pence by Virtue of an Act of Parliament made in the third year of the Reign of His Sacred Majesty King George the Second, etc., for supporting a light-house on the Island or Rock called "Skerries" in St George's Channel. Received also the other lights for London.

10s	10d	Skerries
1	0	Milford
1	0	Scilly
2	0	Lizard
2	0	Eddystone
0	6	Caskets
1	0	Portland
10	10	Dungeness
10	10	Forelands

£2 0 0

Wm Watson,
Collector.

When, in the early part of the nineteenth century, trade between Liverpool and the Americas increased substantially, the Trench family's income increased with it and by the time the lighthouse was taken over by Trinity House the average annual profit from the Skerries was over £12,000.

The Smalls are a cluster of some twenty jagged islets lying twenty miles off a point on the Pembrokeshire coast known as St David's Head. For centuries these rocks had claimed their appalling and monotonous toll of ships and lives, and until they became the property of a Liverpool merchant named Phillips it was not thought possible to mark them. Phillips had for long been distressed by the havoc caused by his property and for years he considered ways and means to set up a light. In 1773 a particularly disastrous shipwreck made him act.

Following what now seems to have become standard practice, Phillips chose an amateur engineer to design and build a lighthouse on the Smalls. Henry Whiteside was a manufacturer of musical instruments and there is no evidence that he had any experience of building at all, let alone that which would seem essential to the erecting of a substantial tower on a small serrated crag of rock twenty miles from land. Yet Whiteside's beacon lit the Smalls for seventy years and was the saviour of many ships and countless lives. After making a detailed survey of the rocks, Whiteside selected one of them as most suitable and designed an iron skeleton tower, 60 feet high, to support a platform on which the keepers' living-quarters and store-rooms would rest; above this was an octagonal lantern-house surrounded by a gallery. When his plan was approved, Whiteside lost no time in landing on the rock with a company of Cornish miners to drill holes that were to take the piles of the structure. The work was dogged by atrocious weather from the start. For some reason the by now established practice of lodging the men in a near-by boat was not followed and a great deal of time was spent in ferrying the work-gang to and from the mainland. On one occasion the men had no sooner landed than a fierce gale blew up, forcing the cutter to retreat from the teeth of the Smalls and make for the open sea. It was two days and nights before it could return and when it did it was a wonder that there was still life on the rock; the marooned men had spent the whole period without food or water, clinging for their lives while exposed to a gale of almost seismic ferocity.

During the early stages of construction Whiteside changed his mind about the use of iron, and the lighthouse, when completed, was supported on nine heavy oak piles. At first the light was attended by two shifts of keepers and, as it happened, one pair of keepers were known to dislike each other intensely. The result of this enmity was tragic and the origin of one of the most famous lighthouse stories of all. One winter the tower was subject to such an atrocious gale that it was impossible to relieve the keepers for four months, during which time one of them was taken ill and died. The other, fearful that if he threw the body into the sea he would be accused of murder, made a shroud for his dead companion and lashed him to the rail of the outer gallery where he remained for several weeks before the relief boat was able to come out. During this time, although in a constant state of near collapse, the surviving keeper never failed to light and maintain the lantern. From then on three keepers were employed on the Smalls lighthouse—a practice which became general in all other isolated stations.

In 1777 Whiteside himself visited the lighthouse to make an inspection and while he was there the usual gale descended on the Smalls which, over a month later, showed no signs of abating. With food, water and fuel almost exhausted, Whiteside wrote the following letter to a friend:

To Mr Williams.
SIR,—Being now in a most distressed and dangerous condition upon the 'Smalls' do hereby trust Providence will bring to your hand this, which prayeth for your immediate assistance to fetch us off the 'Smalls' before the next spring, or we fear we shall perish; our water nearly all gone, our fire quite gone, and our house in a most melancholy manner I doubt not but that you will fetch us from here as fast as possible; we can be put off at some part of the tide almost any weather. I need say no more, but remain your distressed,

Humble servant,
Hy. Whiteside

Another letter was written and signed by Whiteside's companions, the three light-keepers:

We were distressed in a gale of wind upon 13th January, since which have not been able to keep any light; but we could not have kept any light above sixteen nights longer for want of oil and candles which makes us murmur and think we are forgotten.

Ed. Edwards.
G. Adams.
J. Price.

The two letters were put into a bottle with a calm and courteous request to the finder: 'We doubt not but that whoever takes this up will be so merciful as to cause it to be sent to Thomas Williams, Esq., Trelethin, near St David's, Wales.' The bottle was sealed into a cask on which was painted the words, 'Open this and you will find a letter.' The cask was then thrown into the sea in the time-honoured manner and, strangely enough, it came ashore two days later almost outside the door of the addressee where it was found and duly delivered. The note to the finder of the cask gives us a curious little insight into the attitudes of that age. The cask could have drifted a hundred miles before being found and yet the note betrays no urgency, let alone panic. The finder is merely requested to be so merciful as to deliver the bottle to the sender's friend.

In 1831, when the tower had been standing for over fifty years, it was assaulted by a wave of huge proportions which, instead of rolling through the wooden piles, climbed up them with such force that the floor of the keepers' room was torn up and slammed against the ceiling; all the keepers were injured—one so severely that he later died. The damage was repaired and the lighthouse survived for another twenty years before it was replaced by a stone tower. The great lighthouse engineer, Robert Stevenson, visited the Smalls in 1801 and wrote that he was very disappointed with what he saw: 'A raft of timber rudely put together the light of which was seen like the glimmering of a single taper.' Although Trinity House, on the strength of this report, could have compelled the owner to improve the light, they did nothing for another fifty years when, on the death of Phillips, they took over the lease, pulled down the wooden platform and erected a stone tower.

In 1767 it was the turn of the merchants of Belfast to demand a lighthouse. This was to check the depredations to shipping made by the notorious South Rock, three miles off Newcastle, County Down. The demand was made in the form of a petition to the Irish Parliament and it resulted in the report of a Parliamentary Committee that a lighthouse was, indeed, badly needed at South Rock and that the cost of building one would be £5,173. There the matter rested for the next sixteen years while ship after ship ground its timbers over the crags of South Rock. In 1784 another committee examined the proposal and came to exactly the same conclusions except that by now the price had gone up to £6,991 7s 7d. After a further nine years, during which time the only activity on the matter was that shown by the sea, the go-ahead was given. Work started in September 1793 on a 67-foot tower supported on a solid 30-foot-diameter base. It is of interest that the most difficult part of the operation, that of building the base, was done during the winter months. The work was carried out by a foreman, three masons and eighteen labourers.

The original intention was that the granite blocks would be dressed at Wexford, 180 miles away, and carried to the rock by two sloops. On the very first trip there was a violent storm which sunk one of the sloops with its cargo and drove the other to Penzance, this mishap causing considerable delay before the supply service could be continued. In the meantime, Thomas Rogers, the engineer in charge of the works, found another source of granite in a quarry only forty miles from Newcastle and connected to that city by a canal. Here he placed orders for all future supplies. The stones were dressed in Newcastle, two courses at a time.

These courses were temporarily assembled, paper templates being made for the next course and the stones then being shipped out to the rock. Here the courses were bound together by eight vertical iron rods, each 4 inches square, which, forming a circle, were fixed to cast-iron plates at every eighth course. The interior of South Rock lighthouse consists of a coal-room, an oil-room, a kitchen and a living-room connected together by ladders through holes in the floors. Although over 180 years old this tower can still be seen although it ceased acting as a lighthouse in 1877.

It is a fine example of the lasting qualities of eighteenth-century masonry.

The happiest hunting ground of all for the old Cornish wreckers was in the vicinity of Land's End. Two miles to the west lie the Longships, as vicious a cluster of rocks as can be found anywhere in the world; between them and the mainland runs a channel known as Kettle's Bottom. Describing this channel, John Ruskin said 'the whole surface of the sea becomes one dizzy whirl of rushing writhing tortured undirected rage, bounding and crashing and coiling in an anarchy of enormous power'. No wonder that before this point was lit, infant potential wreckers were taught to pray at bedtime: 'God bless father 'n mither an' zend a good ship to shore vore morning.' Their parents organized a regular 'coastguard service' modelled upon the official one but with an entirely different purpose. It has been reported that if a ship was seen to be in difficulties during Divine Service on a Sunday, the news was whispered to the priest who then announced it from the pulpit.

In 1795 a man named Smith was granted the right to impose a toll on passing vessels in return for lighting the Longships, and he built a tower in the centre of a cluster of ragged rocks which bear such strange names as Irish Lady and Armed Knight. Eddystone had been lit long ago and the Lizard relighted with no less than four towers in 1752. Life was getting hard for the wreckers of the Cornish coast and it was soon to be harder still, for within a few years that graveyard of ships was to become the best-lighted coast in the world.

The last part of the eighteenth century also saw significant improvements in lighthouse illumination. On the Mersey, parabolic reflectors had been fitted to some lights, comprising hundreds of mirror fragments set in a plaster of Paris mould formed in a parabolic curve which collected the diffused light from its source and concentrated it in one direction. Before long, highly polished parabolic mirrors of silvered copper had replaced the glass fragments. In about 1780 Aimé Argand invented the burner that is characteristic of oil-lamps today. It comprised a circular wick with a central draught which, surrounded by a glass chimney, gave a brilliant flame. Argand's lamp was a great improvement on the old flat-wick burners and it remained the standard means of domestic lighting for over a hundred years; combined with the parabolic reflector, however, it revolutionized sea-lights by producing a beam of very high intensity from a relatively small light source.[1]

---

[1] According to Argand's younger brother, it was he and not Aimé who invented the lamp and the discovery was accidental. As it is known that Aimé spent years in experimenting with oil-lamps I only offer the story for what it is worth. 'My brother had long been vainly trying to bring his light to bear. A broken-off neck of a flask was lying on the chimney piece; I happened to reach it over the table, and to place it over the circular flame of the lamp; immediately it rose with brilliancy. My brother started from his seat in ecstasy, rushed upon me with a transport of joy, and embraced me with rapture.'

In 1781 the world's first revolving light was installed at Carlsten in Sweden and in the same year spheroidal reflectors were introduced in France. At long last science was taking a hand in lighthouse illumination and the days of coal or tallow-fired beacons were numbered.

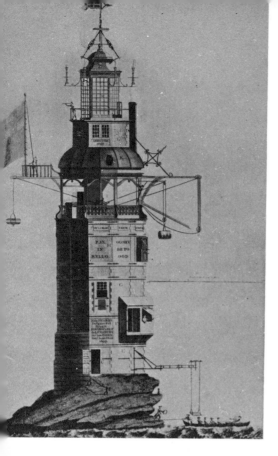

Plate 1a. Winstanley's Tower on Eddystone, finally completed in 1698.

Plate 1b. Rudyerd's tower on Eddystone, completed 1709. The light sections are the granite courses, the dark sections are of wood. The 'ship's mast' runs through the centre.

Plate 2a. Skerryvore lighthouse, 24 miles off the Scottish island of Iona. A masterpiece of marine engineering by Alan Stevenson that took six years to build.

Plate 2b. Vessel on the Longships rocks a short distance from Land's End, 1898.

Plate 3a. Assembling the courses for Douglass's Eddystone lighthouse at the workyard at Plymouth.

Plate 3b. Douglass's Eddystone lighthouse with the stump of Smeaton's tower.

Plate 4. Minot's Ledge lighthouse, completed in 1860.

Plate 5a. Lighthouse on Thimble Shoals, U.S.A. A typical screw-pile tower.

Plate 5b. Fourteen Foot Bank, Delaware Bay. A lighthouse built on a caisson foundation, completed in 1886.

Plate 6a. Relief of Bishop's Rock lighthouse.

Plate 6b. Living-room in a nineteenth-century wave-swept tower.

Plate 7. Beachy Head tower under construction, 1902.

Plate 8a. Fastnet lighthouse, 1906, springs from the base of the rock next to the old (1854) tower on the summit.

Plate 8b. Building the new tower on Fastnet rock.

7

The Early Nineteenth Century

THE GREAT ADVANCES in the building and illuminating of lighthouses made during the eighteenth century were slow in being generally adopted. Many beacons were still in private hands at the beginning of the nineteenth century and their owners, suspecting that the days of private lighthouse keeping were nearing an end, were loathe to replace their coal fires with apparatus that was expensive to install and maintain. The Flat Holme Light in the Bristol Channel was a coal fire until as late as 1822 and the important beacon on the Isle of May, in the Firth of Forth, was fed with coal until 1816. This fire, which burned on top of a tall tower, was tended by three men and was lit nightly for 181 years before the Commissioners of Northern Lights compulsorily purchased it from the Duke of Portland for £60,000 and replaced it with an oil-lamp. In 1810 two ships of the Royal Navy, H.M.S. *Nymphe* and *Pallas*, foundered within sight of each other off Dunbar because both captains mistook the glow from a limekiln for the fire on the Isle of May. The St Bees Head Beacon was also fed by coal until 1822. The tower was 30 feet high and had a ladder on each of the four sides to enable the keeper to avoid the smoke when carrying up the coal. It is recorded that 'each cart [of coal] cost 2s and 1s for driving'. The keeper received wages of 7s a week.

The great lighthouse engineer Robert Stevenson made a tour of English lighthouses in 1801 and the record he made gives some idea of the primitive conditions generally prevailing at the time.

Leaving Carlisle I took Maryport, Workington and Whitehaven harbour lights and the coal fire on St Bees Head on the way to the revolving light upon the Island of Walney. These five lighthouses lie along the coast of Cumberland....

The light upon the pier head of Maryport is from oil with two reflectors. The Workington lights are from candles suspended in two copper lanterns which by means of a tackle are warped out on a pole fixed out with the pier heads. The light upon the pier head at Whitehaven is from oil with one reflector, which is ill-constructed and in bad condition. These lights are shown only during part of flood and ebb tide. . . . St Bees Head light is from coals exposed upon the top of an old tower in an open chauffer, which is at top only two feet diameter . . . so that in storms so small a body of fire cannot be kept up as it ought to be. About one hundred and thirty tons of coal are said to be used here annually, while twice that quantity is consumed at the light of May in the Firth of Forth. This lighthouse of St Bees is private property and is supported by a duty of three halfpence per ton upon vessels trading to certain ports in its vicinity. The duty is farmed and the contractor has the light to uphold.

Walney lighthouse was erected lately in virtue of an Act of Parliament granted to the merchants in Lancaster. The light is from oil with three reflectors each three feet diameter set back to back and made to revolve once in fifteen minutes, so that it is seen alternately light and dark every five minutes and is thereby easily distinguished from St Bees Head light on the one hand and the Liverpool lights on the other. The keeping of this light is very improperly let out in contract to a farmer on the Island of Walney, by which means it becomes only a by-job to one of the contractor's servants and its purposes are almost entirely subverted by the careless manner in which it is kept.[1]

Robert Stevenson was the greatest of all the lighthouse engineers of the nineteenth century, if not in history. His father-in-law, Thomas Smith, was an eminent lighthouse builder and engineer to the Commissioners of Northern Lights, the body responsible for all Scottish lighthouses. At the age of nineteen, Robert was assistant to his father-in-law and was sent by him to superintend the erection of the lighthouse at Little Cumbrae. He consequently succeeded his relative as engineer to the Commissioners and for over a hundred years this position was held by a Stevenson. Robert built a large number of lighthouses, the famous Bell Rock being among them. His son Alan built the classic tower at Skerryvore. He was followed by David who built the North Unst, then came David and Thomas who built Dhu-Heartach and Chicken Rock. They were followed in turn by David and Charles Stevenson who contributed, among others, Rattray Briggs, Sule Skerry and the lights off Flannen Islands. Another member of this distinguished family was Robert Louis Stevenson who, after completing his engineering apprenticeship, abandoned lighthouses in favour of literature.

The Bell Rock, sometimes known as Inchcape Rock, is a sunken ledge of jagged red sandstone lying in the fairway to the Firths of Tay and Forth. It is 2,000 feet long by 330 feet broad and is only visible at low water when its crags rise 6 feet above the waves. Twice a day at high tide it is sub-

[1] *English Lighthouse Tours*, Robert Stevenson, ed. D. Alan Stevenson. London, Nelson, 1946.

merged to a depth of 16 feet and the area around it (which nowhere exceeds three fathoms) is subject to the full undirected fury of the North Sea. Rudyerd's tower, which stood for forty-five years on Eddystone Rock, would not have survived one winter on Bell Rock. Captain Basil Hall in his *Voyages and Travels* says that shipwrecks on the ledge were so frequent that

ships bound for the Forth, in their constant terror of this dangerous reef, were not content with giving it ten or even twelve miles of elbow room, but must needs edge off a little more to the south so as to hug the shore in such a way that, when the wind chopped round to the northward, as it often did, these over-cautious navigators were apt to get embayed in a deep bight to the westward of Fast Castle. If the breeze freshened before they could work out they dearly paid for their apprehensions of the Bell Rock by being driven upon ledges fully as sharp and far more extensive and inevitable. Thus at that time from three to four, and sometimes half a dozen, vessels used to be wrecked every winter within a mile or two of our very door.

That Captain Hall was by no means exaggerating the toll exacted by the Inchcape Rock can be demonstrated by the records—in 1799 no fewer than seventy ships were wrecked upon it.

Farmers living on the rocky coasts near the Bell Rock were said to fence their yards with mahogany and teak and to house their pigs in cedar wood. At times they could wash down their oatmeal porridge with fine claret or carouse drunkenly for days on end with the choicest Cognac. These farms commanded a much higher price than those elsewhere for on them there was more money to be made out of the sea than the land.

The Bell Rock received its name from the famous Scottish legend concerning the good abbot of Aberbrothock and the sinister Sir Ralph the Rover. The story, retold in Robert Southey's famous poem, is that John Gedy, the abbot of Aberbrothock, in the second half of the fourteenth century, hung a bell on Inchcape Rock to warn navigators of its hidden peril.

> And then they knew the perilous rock
> And blest the Abbot of Aberbrothock.

The villain of the story appears in the person of Sir Ralph who, apparently, merely to please an idle whim, removed the bell from Inchcape Rock. Years later, having forgotten all about his little joke, Sir Ralph's ship came across that same rock in the darkness. 'Oh Christ! it is the Inchcape Rock!' he lamented as his ship sailed to its inevitable destruction. And then at the moment of disaster:

> Sir Ralph the Rover tore his hair
> He cursed himself in his despair.

Whether or not there is any basis of truth in the legend of Bell Rock it is certain that the reef had never been adequately marked and that Captain Hall's account of the number of ships it claimed is borne out by Robert Stevenson's narrative of his first landing on the rock.

... meantime, the boatmen were busily employed in searching all the holes and crevices in quest of articles of shipwreck, and by the time the tide overflowed the rock, they had collected upwards of two cwt of old metal, consisting of such things as are used on shipboard . . . such as a hinge and lock of a door, a ship's marking iron, a piece of a ship's caboose . . . a soldier's bayonet, a cannon ball, several pieces of money, a shoe buckle, &c., . . . [and] a piece of kedge anchor, cabin stove, crowbars, &c. . . .

One of the reasons why Bell Rock remained so long unlighted was the peculiar difficulty of building on it. Many engineers had been consulted and they all considered that the construction of a lighthouse there was impossible. Meanwhile the appalling number of ships that fell prey to the Inchcape became a public scandal that forced the Northern Commissioners to take some action. Stevenson was sent to examine the rock and he reported that a lighthouse similar in design to Smeaton's Eddystone tower could be erected. In 1806 an application made to Parliament for a Bill to authorize the work was successful, and Stevenson was appointed engineer to the project with John Rennie as advisory engineer, to be available to Stevenson for consultation should he be needed. In 1807 work began.

As we have seen, the rock was completely submerged twice a day and, as it was eleven miles from the nearest land, there could be no question of ferrying the men out for each workshift. A 40-ton sloop, the *Smeaton*, was built for use as a tender and when construction was started she was moored near the rock and used as the living and sleeping quarters for the thirty to forty men who were variously employed on the works. The men received exceptionally high wages, good rates for overtime and a daily ration of food that included ½ lb of beef, 1 lb of bread, butter, oatmeal, barley, vegetables and three quarts of beer. After working in wet or cold weather, when starting early or finishing later than usual, each man received a glass of rum. As the Bell Rock was liable to be submerged very swiftly, three boats were used so that all the men could leave the rock as one party in the event of a sudden worsening of the weather.

Near to the site selected for the tower a forge was set up and firmly secured to the rock to prevent it being washed away by the tide when the rock was submerged. The establishment of the forge was a good idea for not only could the iron work be made on the spot but tools could be sharpened without being sent ashore.

It often happened [Stevenson relates] when the smith was in the middle of a favourite heat in making some useful article or in sharpening the tools, after the flood-tide had obliged the pickmen to strike work, a sea would come rolling over the rocks, dash out the fire, and endanger his indispensable implement the bellows. If the sea was smooth, while the smith often stood at work knee-deep in water, the tide rose by imperceptible degrees, first cooling the exterior of the fire-place, or hearth, and then quietly blackening and extinguishing the fire from below. [I have] . . . frequently been amused at the perplexing anxiety of the blacksmith when coaxing his fire, and endeavouring to avert the effects of the rising tide.

The year 1807 was confined to preparing the site of the tower and laying the foundations of a barrack that was later to be used to accommodate the men. Near by a flat-bottomed vessel, the *Pharos*, was moored for use as a temporary light.

On 2 September, after Stevenson and the work party had landed on the reef, the wind began to blow hard and a party was sent back in one of the three boats to examine the riding ropes of the *Smeaton*. No sooner had the boat reached its parent ship than the latter broke her moorings and went adrift dragging the boat along with her. It was apparent to Stevenson that with the wind and tide against her the *Smeaton* could not possibly return to the rock until long after it had been submerged by the next tide. Stevenson describes his situation:

In this perilous predicament . . . [I found myself] placed between hope and despair, but certainly the latter was by much the predominant feeling in my mind,—situated upon a sunken rock in the middle of the ocean, which, in the progress of the flood tide, was to be laid under water to a depth of at least twelve feet in a stormy sea. There were this morning thirty-two persons in all upon the rock, with only two boats, whose complement, even in good weather, did not exceed twenty-four sitters.

With the *Smeaton* already three miles to leeward and disappearing rapidly, Stevenson knew that their only chance was to reach the flat-bottomed *Pharos* moored near by, but 'with so much wind, and in so heavy a sea, a complement of eight men for each boat was as much as could with propriety be attempted, so that, in this way, about one-half of our number was unprovided for'.

While the engineer was contemplating their desperate situation, the men, still engrossed in their work, were unaware that anything was wrong and it was only when the forge fire announced knocking-off time by hissing at the advancing sea that they realized that the *Smeaton* was not in its usual place. Then, on the discovery that there were only two boats available instead of the usual three, the clamour of activity gave way to a profound silence as the oncoming tide made its ominous advance towards thirty-two pairs of boots. Having regard to the happy ending of the story, Stevenson's account of his men's reactions to their predicament is almost humorous:

Not a word was uttered by anyone, but all seemed to be calculating their numbers, and looking to each other with evident marks of perplexity depicted in their countenances. The workmen looked steadfastly upon me, and turned occasionally towards the vessel, still far to leeward. All this passed in perfect silence, and the melancholy solemnity of the group made an impression never to be effaced from my mind.

Robert Stevenson could have been forgiven had he repeated the heart-felt cry of Sir Ralph the Rover. He was about to address the men with a suggestion that some of them should get into the boats while the rest hung on the gunwales when the Bell Rock pilot boat was seen approaching. The pilot had come out to deliver letters to the *Smeaton* but on seeing her adrift supposed that all hands were on board considering the state of the weather; he was about to return to shore when he saw the men on Bell Rock. Sixteen were taken off by the pilot while the rest got away in the other two boats. After three drenching hours they finally caught up with the *Smeaton* which took them on board at midnight. So shaken were the men by their narrow escape that on the following morning only eight out the thirty-two were willing to go back to the rock, but the return of this gang in the evening restored the defaulters' courage and work went on as usual next day.

The foundations of the tower were completed in 1808 and in the following year the workmen's barrack was built. The ninetieth and final course was laid in 1810 and the light showed on 1 February 1811. During the forty years that Stevenson lived after building Bell Rock lighthouse not a single ship was lost there. Built before the days of maritime steam navigation, Stevenson's noble tower saw the disappearance of the sailing ship and still glows today, its structure unaltered though having withstood the ravages of time and weather for over 160 years.

In December 1955 a helicopter, making an unauthorized flight to Bell Rock to drop newspapers for the keepers, was destroyed with its crew when it collided with the top of the tower. It damaged the lantern which remained unlit for a week.

The year 1815 saw the first lighting of the Tuskar lighthouse which stands on a low-lying rock off the coast of Wexford in Ireland. It is a granite tower of over 100 feet and was built at a cost of fourteen lives. In October 1812 a huge wave broke over the wooden barrack that housed the workmen and swept it into the sea. Those who were not immediately drowned clung to the rock, and it seems a miracle that anyone could survive such a situation for two days without food, water or shelter. In the result ten men were taken off Tuskar when, at last, a boat was able to reach them. The lighthouse is distinctive as having been put to less altruistic uses than most buildings of its kind. Writing in 1873, J. S. Sloane, engineer to the Irish

Lighthouse Commissioners, gives the following delightful story in his *Manual for Lightkeepers.*

Smuggling and other illicit practices should always be discountenanced by lightkeepers; and, to their honour be it said, the Keepers of the Irish Light Service have been singularly free from any imputation on this score. The only glaring case we have heard of was most graphically described to us on a visit to Wexford in 1862, and we give it almost verbatim as follows: 'The flags were half-mast for the Queen's death when I left Havre in the cutter *Shark*, which I navigated myself. On the fourth morning, about three o'clock, we made the Tuskar Light, where I wore her into the *cothole* and got on shore a large cask and several small kegs of brandy up to 84 over-proof, about 40 pounds of sperm candles, a tin box of playing cards, and several other excisable commodities. To Wisheart and Hunter, the keepers of the lighthouse, I gave especial charge concerning the goods, and promised I would make them a present on my return to claim the property, if I found it untouched. Having lashed all to the ringbolts, and having left all secure, we bore up for Wexford, where I landed, and where we were *over-hauled* by the coastguards and custom-house officers, who, of course, found nothing.

'My next move was to find out when the attending hooker would make her next trip to "Tuskar Rock", and for this purpose I threw myself as carelessly as possible in the way of her skipper, of whom I enquired when he would again run for the rock, as I wished to accompany him. He told me that Tuesday was his day for going there. Ho, Ho! said I. I must remove all on Monday night at farthest. So when Monday came I had a whaleboat lying off "Ballytrent", where, at the time, there was a wooden bathing box, of which I had the key. My crew were men I could depend my life on, and to one of these I gave a candle in a lantern, and I locked him into the box, with strict instructions to watch the coastguards, who always chose the lee side smoking and shelter when on their night patrol; and when the coast was clear, he was to place the lantern to one of the two holes in the box, and thus guide me to safety. I ran from Carrick Rock in 35 minutes, having left at sunset; but judge my surprise when I found the lighthouse lantern remained unlighted. I gained the tower, and on entering it, I found Hunter dead drunk on his back, and Wisheart in the same state on his side, they having "tapped the Admiral" [broached one of the casks]. It was no wonder that the "Royal Yacht" with the King on board, and the British fleet could not discover the Tuskar Light. They saw the Smalls, however, and put in at Milford.

'I gave myself very little trouble on that score, but with the help of the crane which then stood on the rock, I got my brandy and other little matters into the boat, and "lay to" off the shore until late in the night. I saw the light shining from the bathing-box, and knew that I was safe to land. I had a cave prepared, into which I put the brandy, and made all secure.

'It was a wild wet night, and the coastguards came as usual to take shelter under the lee of the bathing-box. My man kept quiet, and after a great deal of desultory conversation heard them say, "Come home, boys: no one will be out this night"; and away they went. So, when he found they were gone, he displayed the light that myself and the boat's crew were so anxiously looking out for.

'I don't know how long the light at Tuskar was out, but it was out long enough to provoke inquiry, which led to the detection of the keepers for allowing the brandy to be landed on the rock, and the dismissal of the coastguards for not keeping a better-look out. Hunter was removed to Halpin's[1] Pool in Dublin, where for years he exercised his abilities as a smith, and Wisheart was removed to Skellig's Rocks, where he was killed by falling over the cliffs while cutting grass for his cow.'

A circular was at once issued from the Ballast Office, Dublin, of which we here give a copy:

BALLAST OFFICE, DUBLIN.
Minutes, Tuesday 23rd October, 1821.

An Examination having taken place into the conduct of Michael Wisheart and Charles Hunter, relative to a smuggling transaction at Tuskar Lighthouse.

IT WAS RESOLVED—'That in consequence of the inattention of Michael Wisheart to his charge at the Tuskar Lighthouse a quantity of contraband goods was deposited on the Rock, and of which he neglected to acquaint the officers of the Board, to remove him from the situation of First Lightkeeper, and that he be placed as second in some other lighthouse.'

RESOLVED—'That Charles Hunter (Assistant Lightkeeper at Tuskar) having permitted the landing of these goods, that he be removed from the situation as a lightkeeper, and that he may be hereafter employed as a working blacksmith (from which employment he had been taken into the Lighthouse Service).'

Australia's first lighthouse of any note was built in 1817. It was a circular stone tower, 76 feet high, supporting a lantern some 15 feet high. It stood 341 feet above sea-level at Macquarie by the entrance to Sydney harbour. There were three resident keepers who were each paid £3 10s 0d per month and a non-resident superintendent who received 5s a day.

In 1818 a novel form of lantern was designed by T. S. Peckston, a British engineer. His proposed system comprised a coal-gas producing plant installed in the lighthouse that would supply gas to the inside of a large metal box rotating within a lens. On each of the four sides of the box small holes were to be punched, each forming a different letter of the alphabet. The gas emerging from the holes would be lit and, as the box revolved slowly, it would, it was thought, spell out a code to passing navigators that would identify the position of the lighthouse. The invention came to nothing mainly because of the difficulty of supplying gas to a rotating container without leakage, but even if this snag had been overcome it is difficult to see what advantage this method of identifying a light would have had over the well-tried flashing beam.

While the British lighthouse authorities were wasting their time with this toy the French were busy with a far more practical development in the shape of the Fresnel dioptric lens. The catoptric reflector had brought about a great improvement in sea-marking but it had certain drawbacks.

[1] George Halpin was the then chief engineer to the Irish Lighthouse Board.

To produce the pencil-like beam that is ideal for lighthouses the ray must be thrown in a horizontal line only. The parabolic reflector only partially achieved this end, thus losing a certain amount of valuable light through diffusion. The French physicist, Augustin Jean Fresnel, designed what can be described as a curtain of prisms in front of the light and centred around a bull's-eye lens. Each ring of prisms projected slightly beyond the next, with the result that all light coming from the source was refracted into a horizontal beam. Fresnel later developed the lens by adding reflecting prisms above and below the refracting prisms and this combination of reflection and refraction is what is known as the catodioptric system. The dioptric lens was first put to a practical application on the Cordouan lighthouse in 1823.

A few miles off the Northumberland coast is a scattered group of rocky and, for the most part, barren islands. They have strange and forbidding names—Piper Gut, Gun Rock, Nameless Rock and the Big and Little Harker Rocks. Before these rocky islets were lit they had an evil reputation among sailors, while the Farne islanders had a more evil reputation still. One old writer says of them: 'When they see a ship in danger they set down on their knees and do pray very devoutly, "Lord, send her to us" . . . but if the ship comes well to port they get up in anger and cry "The devil stick to her, she is away from us".' It seems, though, that these repulsive islanders had some good in them for the *Sailing Directions* for the area issued in 1777 include the offer: 'Dead bodies cast on shore are decently buried gratis.'

On the rocky Farne islet of Longstones there is a fine stone lighthouse which was built in 1826. The first keeper of Longstones light was William Darling, who lived there for many years with his wife, his son and his daughter Grace. The Darlings were a family of lighthouse keepers in two senses of the word for William's father had been appointed keeper of the light on Brownsman isle (one of the Farne Islands) in 1795. When his father died, the mantle of keeper descended upon William who obtained the custodianship of Longstones as soon as it was built and, as was then the custom, moved his family to the isolated rock. In 1838 Grace Darling was twenty-two and, as her mother was ailing and her brother's occupation was on shore, she acted as assistant keeper to her father.

On the night of 6 September, a storm prevented the younger Darling from returning to Longstones and it was the same storm that drove the paddle steamer *Forarshire*, on her way from Hull to Dundee with sixty-three souls, straight onto the north side of Big Harker Rock. The steamer broke up so rapidly that fifty of her people were washed away within minutes of the collision. The other thirteen managed to scramble on to Big Harker where they clung, freezing cold and constantly submerged by the waves that broke over the rock. By morning only nine remained. Four people, including two children, had been torn from the rock by the sea or had fallen from it exhausted.

When daylight came the pitiful group were seen by Grace Darling, who roused her father. Without a moment's consideration of the dangers involved, they launched the flimsy coble, the only boat they had, and rowed through the heaving water towards the maelstrom that centred around the Harker Rocks. The operation of going alongside the reef demanded skill and courage and the two Darlings possessed both. As the flat-bottomed fishing-boat would not hold all the survivors at once, William Darling selected the one woman survivor (she it was, alas, who had seen her two children swept from the rock), one injured man and three others. With her father on the rock helping with the embarkment, it was Grace who handled the oars, keeping the frail boat alongside the jagged rocks which, through one misjudgement on her part, would have torn the coble in two. It was an amazing piece of seamanship more worthy of a master mariner than a girl of twenty-two. The return to the lighthouse was made without mishap and after landing Grace and three of the survivors, William Darling and the two others turned back to Big Harker and rescued those who remained. Half an hour after the operation was completed the life-boat arrived from the mainland and it is inspiring to learn that among the volunteers manning it was Grace's brother, William Brooks Darling.

Grace became a heroine overnight—much to her distaste for she was a shy, retiring girl who had no use for the limelight. Sad to relate, she died of consumption four years later.

8

Heaux de Bréhat and Skerryvore

OR ITS SHEER malevolence the Cornish coast is probably rivalled only by its opposite number—the coast of Brittany. Today the French coast is so well lit that a ship passing along it picks up a new light before losing sight of the last, but this was far from being the situation in the days of sail. With its many scarry islands and wave-swept rocks the coastal edge of Brittany struck terror into the hearts of navigators attempting to steer a middle course between the promontories of Land's End and Ushant. When, in 1833, the French government decided to mark this evil area with a light there was much argument as to where it should be placed, but it was finally decided to build a tall lighthouse on the Heaux de Bréhat, a wave-swept crag that had been the undoing of many a ship. The difficulties of building on this rock were immense. At high water it was almost completely submerged and, being exposed to the full brunt of Atlantic gales, even under the best conditions no more than half a dozen men could work on it and then only for a few hours a day. To add to the hazards, Heaux de Bréhat is swept by strong currents some of which run at up to nine knots.

The engineer Léonce Reynaud was commissioned to undertake the work, and he made a thorough survey of the rock to record the velocities of currents and winds. Heaux de Bréhat is nine miles from the Isle de Bréhat and the latter island was chosen as an operating base. From a little natural harbour a stone jetty was built out for 170 feet and two fleets of small boats were used—one to bring supplies from the mainland to the island, another to convey them to the rock. A total of sixty men were employed in the work, most of them on the island, preparing the woodwork and dressing the granite blocks which arrived in a raw condition from the Ile Grande some thirty miles away.

Heaux de Bréhat is composed of very hard black porphyry, deeply scarred and fissured on its surface, so the first step was to clear off all the cracked and splintered rock to leave a smooth and solid working surface within a circle 38 feet in diameter. Around this circle a trench, 20 inches deep, was hewn to take the first course of stones. This work could only be carried out by a handful of men during the brief periods of low water, and when on the rock they were compelled to work continuously without meal breaks until the rising water drove them into the boats. Near by two rocks surfaced the sea and the space between them was filled up with rubble and masonry to form a rough platform about 13 feet high. On this was built a barrack for the workmen, a forge and a temporary light. The tide was found to be quite unpredictable and it often rose with such rapidity that the men were soaked to the skin before they could get clear. When the trench was completed the first course of stones was laid into it in such a way that they projected a few inches above the surface of the rock, and into this ring of stones, quick-drying cement, which had recently become available, was poured to form a smooth platform on which to build the tower.

This stage of the work was completed by the end of 1835, and in the following year the solid granite base was built up to a height of 39 feet above the highest spring tides. On this base the lighthouse proper was built, the total height of the whole structure being 155 feet. In building Heaux de Bréhat, Reynaud departed from the by then accepted practice of dovetailing each stone to its neighbour but confined himself to securing stones only at the points where the mass of water tended to be more violent. Each course was divided into sections and at these selected points keystones were introduced and firmly secured by granite plugs and wedges. The work took six years and the light shone for the first time in 1839.

While Reynaud was building on Heaux de Bréhat, Alan Stevenson was considering the problem of erecting a lighthouse on Skerryvore, an ill-famed reef lying eleven miles south-west of the Island of Tyree off the Scottish coast. At high water the rock is almost submerged and in winter it is subject to gales that can lift a man off his feet. A proposal for lighting this rock had been put to Robert Stevenson in 1814 and, accompanied by a party of Northern Light Commissioners, he visited Skerryvore to consider its possibilities. One of the party was Sir Walter Scott, who wrote a graphic account of the trip:

Having crept upon the deck about four in the morning, I find we are beating to windward off the Isle of Tyree, with the determination on the part of Mr Stevenson, that his constituents should visit a reef of rocks called Skerry Vhor, where he thought it would be essential to have a lighthouse. Loud remonstrances on the part of the Commissioners, who one and all declare they will subscribe to his opinion, whatever it may be, rather than continue this infernal buffeting.

Quiet perseverance on the part of Mr S, and great kicking, bouncing, and squabbling upon that of the yacht, who seems to like the idea of Skerry Vhor as little as the Commissioners. At length, by dint of exertion, come in sight of this long ridge of rocks (chiefly under water), on which the tide breaks in a most tremendous style. There appear a few low broad rocks at one end of the reef, which is about a mile in length. These are never entirely under water, though the surf dashes over them. To go through all the forms, Hamilton, Duff and I resolve to land upon these rocks in company with Mr Stevenson. Pull through a very heavy swell with great difficulty, and approach a tremendous surf dashing over black, pointed rocks. Our rowers, however, get the boat into a quiet creek between two rocks, where we contrive to land well wetted. I saw nothing remarkable in my way except several seals, which we might have shot, but in the doubtful circumstances of landing we did not care to bring guns. We took possession of the rock in the name of the Commissioners, and generously bestowed our own great names on its crags and creeks. The rock was carefully measured by Mr S. It will be a most desolate position for a lighthouse, the Bell Rock and Eddystone a joke to it, for the nearest land is the wild island of Tyree, at fourteen miles' distance. So much for the Skerry Vhor.

Although Robert Stevenson reported that it was feasible to build a tower on this forbidding reef, the difficulties and the dangers to life were far too obvious and the scheme was shelved.

In 1834 another expedition was made to Skerryvore, this time under the supervision of Robert's son Alan, who mapped the 130 sharp humps of rock of which it is composed. The report he made to the Commissioners was startling to say the least. He proposed to build a tower with a base diameter of 42 feet gradually tapering through 138 feet to a 16-foot diameter at the top (see Plate 2a). It was by far the highest and heaviest light-tower that had ever been contemplated for a wave-swept rock. The solid base section was to extend to 26 feet above the foundation and the cubic content of this base alone was to be double the entire content of Smeaton's Eddystone tower. In more ways than one would the Bell Rock and Eddystone towers be a joke to it.

It is a tribute to Alan Stevenson's ability that at the age of twenty-seven he was made solely responsible for the construction of a tower of 4,308 tons of granite on a nearly submerged rock in mid-ocean and that he was to be entrusted with the then enormous sum of £86,977 of public money with which to do it. Tests carried out on the tower when it was completed indicated that the force of the sea striking it in winter was no less than 2,086 lb per square foot, and during a gale in March 1845 a pressure of 6,083 lb per square foot was recorded! These figures demonstrate not only the immense strength of Alan Stevenson's masterpiece but give a good idea of the appalling conditions under which it was built.

The engineer chose the Island of Tyree as his working base and here he set up work-yards and a barrack for his men. Fortunately there was an abundance of fine quality granite available on the Isle of Mull about twenty miles from Tyree. A jetty was built at Mull and a harbour at Tyree while a specially designed vessel was built to transport the stone and other materials. The Atlantic around Skerryvore is seldom calm so it was not considered prudent to house the men in a floating barrack as had been done at Bell Rock. Instead a house was built on the reef standing on iron stilts 40 feet high to keep it out of reach of the waves. The house comprised of three storeys. The lower one was a kitchen and store-room; next came living and sleeping accommodation for Stevenson and his foreman, while the work force of thirty men occupied the top floor. Access to the rooms was by ladders which passed through holes in the floor. Conditions in the house must have been far from comfortable, for the floor area of the men's room was a mere 200 square feet—about the size of an average living-room on shore—and in this area thirty men ate, slept and spent their leisure time. On the occasions when bad weather prevented work on the rock below, the men would be confined in their uncomfortable and over-crowded quarters for days on end with little else to occupy their minds than the occasional thud of a particularly heavy wave reaching up to hammer on the lowest floor of their house.

Alan Stevenson, who shared the discomforts of his men, gives a good description of life in the barrack:

I spent many a weary day and night—at those times when the sea prevented anyone going down to the rock—anxiously looking for supplies from the shore, and earnestly looking for a change of weather favourable for prosecuting the works. For miles around nothing could be seen but white foaming breakers, and nothing heard but howling winds and lashing waves. At such seasons much of our time was spent in bed, for there alone we had effectual shelter from the winds and spray, which searched every cranny in the walls of the barrack.

The clearing of the surface of the hard gneiss rock proved more difficult than any hitherto encountered. The finest tools were blunted within minutes and the speed of progress was dictated by the time it took to get chisels, picks and drills resharpened. Gunpowder was used but very sparingly as there was no adequate cover from the flying slivers and chips of rock which could kill a man as surely as a bullet at the close range in which they were confined. The building of the barrack was the most hazardous task of all for then the men had to run the risk every morning and evening of landing on and getting off the Atlantic-polished surface of the rocks. Even in high summer it was often impossible to land for days on end and every storm took its toll of material and equipment. No matter how securely they were lashed down, blocks of granite, winches and cranes were torn up and hurled into the sea. The first two seasons were devoted to the building of the barrack and the clearing of the site, and on 7 July

1840 the Duke of Argyll, who had given the Commissioners permission to quarry granite free from his estates near by, made the dangerous trip out to Skerryvore and laid the first stone.

During the following winter a huge and unexpected wave swept over the rock, plucked up the barrack house and cast it into the sea. The house was unoccupied at the time, but one can imagine the feelings of the men as they surveyed the twisted iron piles which were all that remained of their shelter. Stevenson described the apprehensive feelings of his men after this event when depicting life in the second barrack built on Skerryvore:

Our slumbers, too, were at times fearfully interrupted by the sudden pouring of the sea over the roof, the rocking of the house on its pillars, and the spurting of the water through the seams of the doors and windows—symptoms which, to one suddenly aroused from sound sleep, recalled the appalling fate of the former barrack, which had been engulfed in the foam not twenty yards from our dwelling, and for a moment seemed to summon us to a similar fate.

During these noctural tempests no one slept through fear of being caught unawares by another collapse of the barrack and some of the men preferred to spend these nights in the trunk of the lighthouse, sleepless and shivering with the cold and the wet. During one season a storm broke and raged for seven weeks almost incessantly, making it impossible for the supply boat to put out from its harbour. During this period further discomforts were heaped upon the marooned men. Food supplies dwindled to a very low level, fuel was exhausted and, worst blow of all, the supply of tobacco ran out.

These were the conditions under which the Skerryvore lighthouse was built and yet throughout the six years of work there was not one serious accident. The tower was completed in 1843 and was first lit on 1 February 1844. It contains nine floors of one room each, all the rooms measuring 12 feet in diameter. As originally built the rooms were used as a coal store, workshop, store-room, two bedrooms, living-room, oil-store and light-room. Skerryvore lighthouse is an extraordinary feat of engineering combining massive strength with a stately elegance of outline. For over 125 years it has thrown its beam of light over the sea, the while subject to more force of wind and water than any other building could withstand. Built in the face of prodigious difficulties, it is a superb example of engineering skill and serves as a reminder of what can be achieved through sheer perseverance, courage and resourcefulness.

Alan Stevenson was a brilliant engineer who, had he not devoted the whole of his genius to marine construction, would have been as familiar a name today as Brunel or Stephenson. Originally trained for the Church, he decided to join his father as a marine engineer and built nine other lighthouses in addition to his masterpiece at Skerryvore; he also constructed a number of piers and harbours and engineered many river improvements. He possessed fine literary tastes and abilities, having a thorough knowledge of Italian, French, Spanish, Greek and Latin. At the age of forty-five he became paralysed and devoted the rest of his life to making classical translations. *The Times* referred to Skerryvore as one of the four classics of lighthouse building[1] which were described as

. . . the most perfect specimens of modern architecture. Tall and graceful as the minarets of an Eastern mosque, they possess far more solidity and beauty in construction, while, in addition, their form is as appropriate to the purpose for which they were designed as anything ever built by the Greeks.

There was an important development in lighthouse building in 1838 when the first iron screw-pile lighthouse was built on the Maplin Sands in the Thames Estuary by Alexander Mitchell, a blind engineer. Mitchell was the son of the inspector general of barracks in Ireland, and from childhood he had shown a taste and a talent for mathematics. In 1820, when Mitchell was forty years old, his eyesight, always weak, failed him altogether, but this did not prevent him from carrying on with his career as an engineer. Among his numerous inventions was a method of mooring ships through the use of wooden screw piles driven into the bed of the sea, and in 1835 he applied this invention to the building of a lighthouse at the mouth of the river Wyre in Lancashire. The piles were of 3-inch-diameter wood at the bottom ends of which were wide screws, 3 feet in diameter. These were driven into the sand by means of a floating raft with a hole in its centre through which the pile was directed. When the pile reached the sand it was turned by a windlass and screwed home. The Maplin Sands light was supported by eight 5-inch iron piles forming the angles of a hexagon with a ninth, central pile, each of the nine piles having a single turn of a flanged screw 4 feet in diameter. The whole structure was very strongly braced and stood in position for a hundred years before it was undermined and washed away. Each of the piles was screwed to a depth of 22 feet and the nine were put in position in nine consecutive days.

Mitchell patented his invention in 1842 and screw-pile lights were built all over the world but particularly in the United States where they found especial favour. Once the screw-pile method became established it was applied to more extensive undertakings, such as breakwaters, piers, viaducts and bridges. When Mitchell's patent expired he was granted an extension of a further fifteen years in view of the merits of his invention.

[1] The other three presumably being Eddystone, Bell Rock and Heaux de Bréhat.

9

The Age of Engineering Developments

IN THE SAME year that the Maplin Sands light was established, one of
the most famous lighthouses in the English Channel was raised at St
Catherine's Point on the Isle of Wight. Built of ashlar stone, it was
originally a three-tier octagon of a most elegant design. The first light had
been shown from this point early in the fourteenth century when a
benevolent knight built a chantry on St Catherine's Downs and provided
an endowment for a priest to 'chant Masses and maintain a burning light
at night for the safety of mariners'.

The octagonal tower was found to be too high as mist often shrouded the
lantern, so in 1875 20 feet were removed from the top tier and 23 feet from
the middle resulting in a rather squat tower. In 1932 a fog signal house was
annexed to the older tower and the result is charming. The combined
buildings are known locally as the 'Cow and the Calf'. St Catherine's was
one of the first British lighthouses to be lit by electricity and its present
intensity is 5,250,000 candle power.

An extraordinary feat of engineering was performed in September 1841
when the lighthouse on the north end of Sunderland pier was moved in its
entirety to the extremity of the new eastern extension of the pier—a
distance of over 500 feet—the whole operation being carried out without
interrupting the illumination of the tower. The Commissioners of the
River Wear at first intended pulling down the lighthouse and re-erecting
it, but they were approached by a civil engineer named Murray with a
plan for shifting it complete. First the masonry at the base was cut through
and timbers inserted through the building and projecting for 7 feet at
either end. Above, and at right angles to them, another tier of timbers was
inserted in a like manner to make a 20-foot-square base or cradle which in

turn was supported by a huge wagon with 250 wheels, each 6 feet in diameter. From the old site to the new, six lines of railway were laid and the lighthouse, lantern, keepers and all were traversed to their new position. It was at first intended to move the burden with powerful screws, but the move was eventually made with a windlass and ropes worked by thirty men. The tower was an octagonal one and its shaft was tied for the move with iron bands around timber braces that supported the eight sides from the cradle up to the cornice. The operation went smoothly and when it was completed not a crack was found in the building.

During the same year a lighthouse was built in about as unlikely a spot as one could imagine a lighthouse to be, for it towered 105 feet above Belgrave Place, in Pimlico, London. It was built in Bramah and Robinson's Works, to be taken to pieces and re-erected at Morant Point on the west coast of Jamaica. Made entirely of 1-inch iron plates, it was eventually sunk into 15 feet of solid rock. To insulate the iron rooms from the heat of the Jamaican sun the whole structure was lined with slate with a cellular space between the slate and iron of $1\frac{1}{2}$ inches. A most bizarre addition was made in the form of a lightning conductor running down the metal sides which was, said *The* London *Times*, 'to convey the electric fluid to the ground'. The lighthouse was designed, built, dismantled and shipped in under three months.

Another important advance in marine engineering was made in 1845 when Dr Laurence Potts demonstrated the pneumatic pile for the first time. This was but one invention of this extraordinary and brilliant man. A practising physician who specialized in diseases of the spine, a pioneer of psychology and a well-known mineralogist, he was responsible for many minor inventions and had taken out a patent for conveying letters on a wire railway. His scheme was that the church spires of all towns and villages could be interconnected with wires along which could be sent tiny carriages containing the mail. His idea for sinking submarine piles through atmospheric pressure was ingenious in its simplicity. It was proposed to erect a beacon to mark the Goodwin Sands and it was here that Potts first demonstrated his invention. An iron tube, 2 feet 6 inches in diameter, was placed perpendicularly on the sea-bed with its other end protruding above the surface of the water. This end was closed with an air-tight cap and a powerful pump exhausted the air from the tube, causing the sand and shingle at the bottom to be forced up through the pipe by the pressure of the atmosphere—the rush of water from below breaking up the soil and undermining the lower edge of the pile. The pile descended by its own gravity assisted by the pressure of air at the closed end. When the tube was full the contents were pumped out, a further length attached to it, and the process repeated. The first pile driven into the Goodwins was sunk to a depth of 22 feet in just over two hours. Although, for some reason, the

Goodwin Sands beacon was not proceeded with for another two years, Potts's method was used for building beacons at Buxey, Shingles, the Girdler, Margate and at many other places.

The invention was taken up and developed by Charles Fox of the famous civil engineering firm of Fox and Henderson and was widely used for sinking the piles of railway bridges. By 1850 tubes of up to 10 feet diameter were being used. Potts's invention was never a financial success although he gave up medicine and devoted all of his time and most of his fortune to its development; but it had one very important result that had a great effect on marine and river engineering and on lighthouse building in particular. When the Rochester bridge was under construction in 1850 it was intended to use Potts's method for building the piers, but the engineer in charge, one J. Hughes, discovered that the bed of the river was blocked with the remains of a very ancient bridge and his cylinders would not penetrate the stone obstruction. It occurred to Hughes to reverse the process—i.e., to pump air *into* the cylinders so that men could get inside them and clear away the obstacle. An air lock was provided for access to the cylinders and it was found that as the material was cleared away the pipe sunk through its own weight.

Potts's method for driving piles was thus developed into the means of sinking caissons into the ocean-bed large enough to bear the weight of tall granite towers.

In 1854 Britain was at war with Russia, and to prevent the Russian fleet from sailing around Scotland's northern coast, the British Navy kept up a constant patrol of the northern extremities of Great Britain's coastline. It was to protect the British warships from the ocean hazards that litter the coast of the Shetlands that the North Unst lighthouse was built. This sea-light, then, was the first of the few that were called into being through the needs of war rather than those of peaceful trade. It is an unfortunate fact that man's energy multiplies when channelled into the means of conflict and destruction, for during times of war great feats of engineering are performed in a fraction of the time that they would take during times of peace. Thus it was that the first North Unst lighthouse was built in the remarkable time of twenty-six days and under the most adverse weather conditions. The place chosen by the engineers to erect this most northerly light in the British Isles was on Muckle Flugger, a crag of rock which rises to 196 feet above high water. Despite its great height, the waves of the Atlantic assault Muckle Flugger with such violence that its very summit is frequently drenched with water. Even this is not the limit of the power of the waves for they have been known to envelop the present lantern which is 260 feet above high-water level.

The first difficulty encountered by the engineers was the steepness of the rock; to reach its summit the men had to rope themselves together and attack the overhanging crags as they would on a mountain. Work started in September 1854, in the face of a severe winter. The site for the light was hewn out of the near iron-hard rock with hammers, chisels and wedges, then a flight of steps was carved in the side of the peak to give access to the summit for men and materials. Tackles and sheerlegs were manhandled up the steep sides of the rock and when these were in place the heavier pieces of equipment, stores and material, amounting to over 120 tons' weight, were hauled up. The first materials were landed on 14 September and by 11 October Muckle Flugger was lit.

The building was never intended to be more than a temporary one to serve immediate needs, but with the establishment of a level site and the steps on the rock's flank, it was decided to erect a masonry building for the guidance of ships passing round the Scottish coast between the North Sea and the Atlantic. The permanent lighthouse was to be begun in the following year and a gang of workmen were persuaded to remain on the rock throughout the winter to enlarge the site and prepare the foundations. To withstand the known force of the sea at Muckle Flugger a large iron house was built to accommodate the men and their stores, and within it they made themselves comfortable, quite confident that they were immune from the fury of the sea some 200 feet below. One morning in December while the men were preparing breakfast this confidence was shattered when a huge wave rushed up the rock like an express train to deal a steam-hammer blow on the side of their dwelling. The door flew open and admitted a three-foot high wall of water that swirled around the room before retreating through the door, sucking with it everything movable. Before the drenched men had had time to close the door, an even bigger rush of water seethed around their legs to be followed seconds later by a reverberating boom as another mass dealt a blow to the iron roof that would have done justice to Thor.

It seems almost unbelievable that waves can climb to a height of 200 feet, but it must be remembered that those that strike Muckle Flugger do so at the end of an unimpeded run of hundreds of miles of open sea. When the news of this incident was brought to the engineers they decided to build a massive stone wall around the proposed lighthouse and it is as well that they did, for on one occasion a heavy wave bounded up the rock, against and over the wall, to smash open the lighthouse door which weighs nearly a ton. A few seas like that one, uninterrupted by the wall, would have made short work of the tower.

Another lighthouse of that period is the one on the Grand Barge d'Olonne, a wave-swept rock nearly two miles from the French coast. The ferocity of the wind and the sea met with here by the engineers was such that the building took five years to complete; during that time only 1,960 hours were worked—an average of a little over an hour a day. This tower is of granite blocks mortised and tenoned together.

On the other side of the Atlantic, Cape Race in Newfoundland received its first lighthouse in 1856; this was a cylindrical cast-iron tower perched on the edge of a cliff, 87 feet above the sea. The result of a joint effort between the Newfoundland and the British Governments, it was maintained by the latter who levied a due of one-sixteenth of a penny per ton on all vessels passing the light. Some fifty years later the lighthouse was handed over to the Canadian Government who abolished the light-dues. By the end of the nineteenth century shipping to and from Canada had so increased that it was decided to build a taller and more powerful beacon on Cape Race; in consequence a lighthouse was built which then ranked as the finest in the world. Built of reinforced concrete the tower was 100 feet high and carried an incandescent oil burner and mantle of 1,100,000 candle-power.

Eighty-five miles due east of Nova Scotia, and directly across the shipping lanes, lies Sable Island, a desolate stretch of land some twenty-two miles long by one mile wide. The danger of Sable Island lies not so much in the isle itself as in the many submerged sand-banks which extend from its shores. Even small ships do not approach within sixteen miles of the island, for navigators know that even if they pass safely over one bar they will surely come to grief on another. During the nineteenth century alone over 150 ships were wrecked on Sable Island which now shows two lights.

The light on the western end of the island was built in 1873 at a point well inland for it was realized that the shore was being rapidly eroded by the ocean. Unfortunately, the speed of the erosion was underestimated and in 1881 a whole area of 1,400 feet long by 70 feet wide was carried away in a single storm with the result that the tower was left fully exposed to the sea which was still advancing. The winter of 1882 was even more severe and the constant swaying and vibrating of the tower convinced the keepers that its collapse was imminent if it was exposed to a gale. It was decided to dismantle the lighthouse and to re-erect it in a safer place and with each day bringing worse weather a battle for the tower was waged between the men and the sea. The lantern and superstructure were got away safely when a wave of particular violence struck the side of the building which trembled and swayed and plunged into the sea.

No chances were taken in placing the second light, which was built over 2,000 yards from the island's western extremity and on a knoll some 20 feet above sea-level. It is an octagonal building of ferro-concrete, 97 feet high and was brought into service in 1888. The light on the eastern end of Sable Island is also an octagonal tower and was built in 1873.

The slender outline of the lighthouse on Bishop's Rock, climbing to 110 feet above the surface of the sea, has been familiar to transatlantic voyagers for over a century. This rock, a granite peak lying seven miles south-west of the Scillies, is about 155 feet long by 52 feet wide and its sides drop almost sheer to the ocean bed 150 feet below. Like the Wolf Rock it is a fearful obstacle to the dense and constant maritime traffic that plies the English Channel; its toll of wrecks is as great as any other notorious rock in the area. Among the hundreds of vessels resting at its foot and commemorated by its stone tower are three ships of Sir Cloudesley Shovell's fleet which were driven onto it in 1707. The fleet was returning from Lisbon when, on 22 October, in cloudy weather with a strong westerly wind, it came to soundings off the Scilly Islands. Here it was set to the north by the action of the powerful current and the Admiral's flagship *Association*, together with *Eagle* and *Romney*, was smashed to pieces on the granite sides of the Bishop. Over two thousand men drowned in the space of a few minutes, and although Sir Cloudesley was alive when his body was washed ashore in Porthellick Cove he was not destined to survive. The wrecking community of the Cornish coast were astir on the shore and the admiral's unconscious body was found by a woman who dispatched him with a stone before taking an emerald ring from his finger. The body was subsequently found, taken on board the *Salisbury*, and finally buried in Westminster Abbey. Some writers have thrown doubt on this particularly gruesome episode in the history of wrecking but it is on record that the woman confessed her crime to a clergyman some thirty years later. He retrieved the ring and returned it to Shovell's descendants.

The first lighthouse to be set up on Bishop's Rock was an open structure consisting of cast-iron legs sunk into the solid granite and braced with wrought-iron ties and stays; this supported an iron platform to house the light and was thought at the time to be the only feasible way of displaying a light at this violent place, for wind-pressure tests had sometimes indicated a pressure of 7,000 pounds per square foot. A tower built to withstand such enormous forces, it was thought, would be too mighty to be practicable, while an iron-legged platform would offer no resistance to the wind and the waves. The structure took nearly three years to build and by February 1850 it was complete except for the light. It faced its first real test on the night of 5 February when a storm of cataclysmic fury swept in from the north-west and fell upon the 94-foot iron tower. It failed, for in the morning nothing remained but a few stumps of cast iron sticking up from the rock.

The most essential quality required by a successful engineer is perseverance, and the engineer in charge of the Bishop's Rock project, Nicholas Douglass, was a very determined man indeed. To have almost completed a three-year project in a veritable maelstrom of foam and surf only to find it completely snatched away during the course of a single night would have dismayed the most stoical of engineers. Douglass's face on the morning after the storm must have been a study, but his dismay was short-lived.

It had been conclusively proved that an openwork structure could not survive on this gale-torn rock; therefore, Douglass argued, the only possible alternative was a masonry tower however formidable might appear the problems of building it. Lighthouse building is as lighthouse building does.

Douglass made a lengthy and careful examination of the rock to select a suitable site for a tower, with the result that he learned that he had no choice at all. There was but one possible place and that, unfortunately, was a foot below sea-level and could only be kept dry during the calmest weather. The first step, therefore, was to build a stone coffer-dam around this site and pump it dry. While this work was in progress Douglass established a base of operations on a near-by islet and here a barrack was built to house the men; it was to here that the rough granite blocks were sent to be shaped by masons before being transported to the rock for erection. Seven years of hard labour were put in at Bishop's Rock before the 120-foot-high tower was lit in 1858.

There occurred in 1860 an incident which typifies the steadfastness and courage of the lighthouse-keeping breed. In this case the keepers calmly carried on with their duties while their tower was literally falling down around them. The lighthouse concerned was built in 1848 at a point called Double Stanners, near Lytham in Lancashire. Situated near high-water mark the tower, 72 feet high, exhibited two fixed lights. The night of 7 January 1863 brought great gales upon the English coast and, buffeted by a strong wind and heavy seas, Lytham lighthouse began to vibrate ominously. Halfway through the night the tide withdrew and one of the keepers inspected the building from the outside. What he found was disturbing to say the least, for the sea had undermined the north corner to the extent of working some of the masonry out and laying bare the foundations to their very bottom. The men could quite easily have left the light to burn by itself for the few hours of darkness that remained, but their main concern was to remove everything in the building that was not essential to showing the light and to carry it to a safe place. This work went on until daybreak when the tide again surrounded the lighthouse, further undermining it to the extent that it was practically balancing on a knife-edge. That evening the keepers went back and the light shone as usual. In the morning it was extinguished for the last time. With the tower on the very verge of collapse, the keepers spent the morning dismantling the lamp and carrying away the lenses, reflectors and lighting apparatus. They even salvaged the oil from the cisterns, gaining access to it through a breach made by the tide in the ground floor. By 11 a.m. everything had been carried to a safe place and at noon the south corner foundation gave way and Lytham lighthouse collapsed.

A few years after this disaster the lighthouse on Calf Rock at the entrance to Bantry Bay on the west coast of Ireland was swept into the sea during a violent gale. The keepers, feeling the tower tremble, evacuated the building in the nick of time and took shelter in a hollow on the lee-side of the rock. Here they remained for twelve days before a boat could come to their rescue.

The practice of establishing flashing, self-identifying lights meant a severe decline in the fortunes of wreckers, although a document dated 14 March 1870 indicates that at least one of them recouped his losses by following the axiom of 'if you can't beat 'em, join 'em'. The letter was from the deputy inspector of lighthouses in the Bahamas to the Governor of Bahamas Colony, and reads:

Latterly several vessels have gone ashore very near the [Gun Cay] lightstation, which after great consideration has induced me to address you this letter. In the Court of Inquiry into the loss of a vessel, do the Nautical Assessors question the master relative to the number of seconds between the revolutions of the light? Is it seen every thirty or ninety seconds? If it should be thirty, then anyone might easily mistake it for the light on Carysfort Reef and so keep to the eastward, thereby running aground. While I do not wish to raise any suspicion on the keepers in regard to the irregularity of the timing of the light, I feel I should appraise Your Excellency that the Principal Keeper has married into a family of notorious and unscrupulous wreckers, residing at Bimini a few miles away.

The governor was very wise in taking this remarkable intelligence seriously. When the keeper was transferred the number of wrecks at Gun Cay decreased.

Not far from Bishop's Rock there lies, at about eight miles from Land's End, the dreadful Wolf Rock—an ancient menace to sailors but a source of joy to the Cornish wreckers, for in the darkness or in fog any ship taking the short cut around the toe of England ran a heavy risk of being driven towards the Wolf by wind and current to be torn to pieces by its sharp fangs. On the reef there was once a hollow rock into which the waves washed, compressing the air; when the air escaped it produced a long melancholy howl like that of a wolf and it was from this wail that the rock got its name. The distinctive cry of the Wolf became so familiar to navigators that upon hearing it they gave the reef a wide berth. This was not to the liking of the wreckers. One day a gang of them took a boatload of boulders from the mainland and filled up the hole. Thereafter business was brisk. After an abortive attempt by the more civilized coast-dwellers to re-open the hole it was decided to recreate the warning howl of the wolf by artificial means. A wolf's head, with open jaws, was cast in copper, so designed to produce a wail—weather permitting. This device was never set up—probably because its makers discovered that any noise produced would be practically inaudible to passing ships until too late. Some years after this episode Trinity House took a hand in the problem of Wolf Rock.

A thick oak shaft was driven into its back and upon it was set a coloured sphere to act as a day-mark. The sea made short work of this—as it did a long succession of iron shafts that were set up subsequently. The last of these was nine inches in diameter, but even this was broken off short by the first severe storm. Finally a low iron cone erected to support the sphere withstood the elements for many years. In 1861 the Brethren decided that impossible though the task might appear, a light tower had to be built on Wolf Rock; they sent an engineer, James Nicholas Douglass, to make a survey. Douglass was thirty-five at the time and a very experienced lighthouse engineer. The son of Nicholas Douglass, the superintendent engineer to the Corporation who had built on Bishop's Rock, he had been resident engineer for the Gun Fleet Pile lighthouse and, in 1859, he had built the tower on the Smalls.

When Douglass made his survey he got a taste of what he was up against. After a difficult landing he made his examination and signalled the boat to return for him; but at that very moment the weather took a turn for the worse, making it impossible for the boat to approach. With the tide rising alarmingly it was fortunate for Douglass that he had brought one end of a life-line with him, the other end being secured to the boat. This he tied about his waist and jumped into the sea; he was taken safely aboard, though after a very rough haul. The result of this reconnaissance allowed Douglass to convince the Trinity House Brethren that a tower could be built on Wolf Rock and he was instructed to set to work on a design. The drawings he produced followed the, by then, conventional lines. Solid at its base the tower, which has withstood over a century of the ocean's buffetings, rises 135 feet above sea-level; it is built of granite blocks tied together with joggles.

The stone masons first landed on the rock in March 1862 to begin the dangerous work of preparing the surface of the reef and cutting into it the dovetails which were to receive the first course of stones. Meanwhile another gang of masons were constructing a stone landing stage to accommodate a derrick for the lifting of the heavy granite blocks from the supply boat to the rock. Work was restricted to the very brief periods of low water; even then the men were continually drenched by the waves and in constant danger of being swept into the sea. During the first season the average working time amounted to less than an hour a day and at the end of these short periods the men were taken off the rock almost exhausted by the effort of alternately clinging to a handhold for their lives and chipping at the hard gneiss with hammer and chisel. To protect them from being swept away, iron stakes were driven into the rock at frequent intervals with life-lines fastened to them which trailed across the surface of the reef, each man being ordered to keep one of the ropes within reach. A Cornish fisherman, whose experience of the coast enabled him to judge the power of approaching breakers, was stationed as a look-out and, in addition, the men were compelled to wear lifejackets at all times. At a signal from the look-out each man would grasp his life-line and throw himself face downward on the reef until the wave had passed over him. It was no wonder that under such conditions the progress of the work was slow and that by the end of the third working season only two courses of masonry were completed. By the end of 1865 the tower had risen beyond the reach of the sea and from then onwards progress was rapid—even so it took another three years to finish the work, the last stone being laid on 19 July 1869 after eight years of toil. During this time 296 landings were made on Wolf Rock and 1,814 hours worked.

The designers and builders of lighthouses bear heavy responsibilities. Their main concern is that the lights they establish shine out at night with absolute regularity, for an unreliable light can be a far worse hazard than the one upon which it stands. It is not surprising then that lighthouse engineers are conservative people who, like doctors, are loathe to introduce new methods until they have been thoroughly proved. Trinity House was the first lighthouse authority to employ electric light and it took no less a person than Faraday to overcome the Brethren's reluctance to be first in the field. The lighthouse selected was the South Foreland light and a magneto and arc lamp were installed there in 1859. In order to compare the qualities of the electric arc with the then conventional oil-lamp the two methods of lighting were exhibited simultaneously so that passing ships could report on the comparative qualities of each. It was said that on a clear night the electric arc could be seen for twenty-seven miles, which would be quite possible from a masthead if its height, combined with that of the tower, was 300 feet.

The French turned to electric lighting in 1863 with the installation of an arc lamp in Cape Hève lighthouse that produced a light of 60,000 candle power. This was considered so powerful at the time that the French government instituted a series of experiments with electric arcs which, by 1881, produced a light of 1,270,000 candle power.

The introduction of electric light into lighthouses was the first step in transforming the light-keeper from an unskilled man to the skilled technician he is today. The principal keeper at an electrically lighted house became known in the 1870s as the engineer and was excused watches, although he was compelled to visit the lantern-room and engine-room at least once during each four-hour watch when the lamp was alight. His assistants took equal watches of four hours on and four off in the engine-room and lantern-room, the watches being alternating. Two sets of engines and two sets of boilers were worked alternately, one each week; and in case of a mechanical breakdown, oil-lamps were kept ready trimmed and lighted and focused for one hour each week. This test was, of course, carried out in daylight to avoid interfering with the regular, electric, light.

Coal-gas, which had been first tried out in 1837 at the pier light of Troon in Ayrshire, gradually replaced oil at many shore stations where gas supplies were available. The Baily (Ireland) lighthouse became the most powerful in the world when, in 1865, it was equipped with a multi-jet burner supplied with coal-gas made in the lighthouse itself. This apparatus was designed and built by John Wigham who later invented an intermittent gas-light which was operated by a clockwork mechanism working a gas valve. Trinity House were offered the use of Wigham's invention for a nominal royalty of a shilling a year but, refusing to commit themselves to this arrangement, the Brethren copied the apparatus. As a result they were sued by Wigham's firm and required to pay £2,500 in compensation.

A Lighthouse Built on Sand

AS AN EXAMPLE of sheer, dogged perseverance the building of the lighthouse of Ar-men has few equals in engineering history—its building occupied no less than fifteen years, nine of which were spent in making the foundation and the base. On the western extremity of the *dèpartement* of Finistère in north-west France lies the island of Sein, the western side of which trails off into a series of mostly submerged reefs running in a line almost perpendicular to the direction of the tidal currents. As a result the rocks are surrounded by powerful and rapid currents which dash the sea against them with great violence.

As through the first half of the nineteenth century the flow of ships crossing the Bay of Biscay increased, so did the number of them coming to grief on the reefs, and by 1860 it had become a matter of extreme urgency to light this dangerous spot. In April 1860 it was decided by the French Lighthouse Board that, difficult though the task would be, it was imperative to build a first-order lighthouse on one of these unsubmerged rocks and a reconnaissance of the area was carried out. Of the three possible sites —the rocks called Madion, Schomeor and Ar-men—the last-named was chosen as the most suitable. In the centre of a vortex of water, Ar-men, at low tide projecting a mere 5 feet above the surface, offered a foundation 25 by 45 feet. Every inch of the smaller dimension was required to raise the high tower that was needed.

Work started in 1867 with the boring of fifty-five holes to take the stanchions and wrought-iron gudgeons that were to serve the dual purpose of fixing the masonry to the rock while binding together the various fissures in the rock itself. At the end of the first season only seven landings had been made in spite of the greatest efforts and only fifteen holes were bored. The next season allowed sixteen landings and the completion of the fifty-five borings. The net result of two years was twenty-six hours' work; so it was no wonder that Ar-men lighthouse was fourteen years building. Day after day, often week after week, the men would wait at their depot with a boatload of stones for conditions that would allow them to get onto the rock. When they would work feverishly to fix as many blocks as they could before the sea drove them off again. The solid cylindrical foundation, 24 feet in diameter and 18 feet high, took seven years to build.

The base of the tower occupied a further year and in 1876, nine years after the start of the work, the lighthouse proper was begun. Rising through eight storeys to a height of 100 feet, it tapers from a diameter of 21½ feet at its base to 16½ feet at the top; its walls diminishing in thickness from no less than 5½ feet at the bottom to 2½ feet at the lantern-house. The building of this tower occupied a further five years and a fixed white light of the first order was lit in 1881.

While the French engineers were playing their waiting game with the elements at Ar-men, David and Thomas Stevenson were engaged in the arduous and dangerous task of subduing the ominously named Dhu-Heartach Rock, some nineteen and a half miles from the Skerryvore. Lying as it does at the entrance to the Irish Channel, this dangerous reef was dreaded by generations of seafarers sailing Britain's coastal waters. For years the Commissioners of Northern Lights had been urged to place a light on the whale-like back of Dhu-Heartach but it was not until 1867 that anything was done. Like Skerryvore, Dhu-Heartach receives the full force of rollers that have travelled unimpeded for hundreds of miles, and when they reach the rock they burst upon it with almost unimaginable force. The power of the sea around Dhu-Heartach was demonstrated when the tower had reached a height of 36 feet above high water. A huge wave enveloped the works, tearing away eleven granite blocks all dovetailed together to form a mass weighing over 22 tons. As there was no lack of space on the reef it was decided to build a barrack for the men who would then be able to spend the entire season at the works. This took the form of an iron house on piles similar in design to the one that had served on Skerryvore. Its construction took up the whole of the first two seasons of work, the rock being so difficult of access that only thirty-eight landings could be made.

August 20, 1868, having been fixed as the last working day of the second season, Alexander Brebner, the resident engineer, was sent out to the reef to make a final inspection and to bring the men back to the mainland. He arrived on the rock on a calm, genial day and, on his own responsibility, he made the decision to delay the evacuation for a few more days to carry on with the work. The fair weather continued into the night when Brebner and his gang of thirteen men retired to their newly completed shelter. They were awakened by the first of a series of reverberating blows on the roof of the iron house as the ocean did its utmost to sweep it off the rock. The legs of the barrack now rose from a veritable maelstrom of boiling surf and as one foam-crested roller swept over the shelter it was immediately followed by another. For five days the men huddled in the barrack expecting every moment to be swept into the sea. Fear and noise made sleep impossible. The entrance to the house was a heavy iron trapdoor in the floor, bolted with a stout iron bar. At one point a particularly powerful wave lunged 55 feet upwards, smashed open the trapdoor and flooded the room. When it retreated it took with it the little store of food that remained and left the soaking men shivering with fright as well as cold.

On shore the Stevensons were in a state of much anxiety at the prospect of the loss of fourteen of their men and furious with Brebner for staying on the rock contrary to orders. Instructions were issued that the tender should stand by with steam raised and, at the first sign of a lull in the weather, dash out to the rock and take off the men. Eventually Brebner and his gang were brought back to the mainland unharmed.

The working season of 1869 brought exceptionally mild weather and the men were able to take up residence in their house in April, working, with Sundays excepted, every day until 3 September. When the foundations were prepared the solid base of the tower, alone weighing 1,840 tons, was built up to a height of 64 feet above high water. In 1871 the lighthouse was completed and the light, a fixed dioptric of the first order, shone out on 1 November 1872. It is on record that a section of the lightning conductor on the side of the building was once torn away by the waves at a height of 92 feet above high water. The keepers of Dhu-Heartach light must have nerves of steel.

The estuary of the Weser river is surrounded by numerous shoals and sandbanks that made the passage to Bremerhaven an extremely hazardous one until the bordering states of Prussia, Bremen and Oldenburg agreed between them to light the channel. At first it was decided to place a lightship at the entrance to the Weser, but upon inspection it was found that the shifting nature of the sands made it impossible to moor a vessel there. The only alternative was to build a stone light tower on the sandy bed of the ocean—a task never before attempted. After selecting the Rothersand shoal as a site for the lighthouse, the three allied states empowered Bremen to undertake the project so, in 1878, the lighthouse establishment of that state approached the Harkoort Company of Duisburg asking them if they would undertake the work at their own risk—that is, that if they failed in the undertaking they would not be paid. As the task of building a masonry tower on a subaqueous sand foundation had never before been attempted it is surprising that Harkoort's agreed to this proposal.

The company's plan, as daring as it was original, was to build a massive iron caisson which would be floated to the site, sunk and filled with concrete, thus creating an artificial rock on which to build the tower. While the drawings were in preparation there was an unexpected development when Harkoort's chief engineer resigned his post and, with two other engineers, formed a rival company to tender for the contract. Harkoort's figure was £24,025 but the younger company, appropriating the idea of its parent, secured the deal with a bid of £22,750.

The caisson, measuring 35 feet in diameter, was built during the winter of 1880–81 and on 2 May, with a dead calm sea, it was towed to the site by two tug boats. There it immediately parted from its towline to drift ashore with the ebb tide. In the morning, after floating off with high water, it was again secured by the tugs and returned to the site. Four days after leaving harbour, it was sunk onto the ocean-bed by the rather haphazard method of removing a large wooden bung in its bottom—an operation that caused the water to rush in with such force that the great iron cylinder behaved like a spinning top. At dusk it reached the ocean-bed safely and a gang of men in the charge of an engineer were left on the caisson for the night while the rest retired to the constructional steamer moored near by.

During the night a heavy fog descended on the Rothersand and, as the tide rose, the men sleeping on the caisson were rudely awakened when it suddenly lurched over to an alarming degree hurling them out of their berths. In an attempt to straighten the caisson the men moved over to the elevated side, but to their horror they observed the list slowly increasing until at last they could not keep their feet. Meanwhile the depressed top edge was nearing the surface of the sea. When the fog lifted the plight of the party was seen by the crew of the steamer who sent boats to take the men off. For four days the caisson was left to its fate until the action of the flood current righted it. By mid-May the wall of the caisson had been built up by a further 6 feet but then a month of heavy storms made more work impossible. When the working party returned on 14 June they found that the scour caused by the storms had sunk the caisson into the sand to a depth of 17 feet. The concrete filling was then started and the water in the air-shaft and working-chamber was blown out by compressed air. By the end of September, with the iron barrel sunk to a depth of 43 feet, the approach of winter compelled the working party to return to the shore. Unfortunately the work was behind schedule and the caisson was unfit to face the winter storms. The brick lining had not been started and the concrete filling was only up to the level of the ocean-bed. Worst of all, the iron shell of the cylinder was only braced with cross-timbers which were quite inadequate to withstand the storms of the North Sea. On the morning of 13 October a shore look-out, observing the structure through a glass, was amazed to see it suddenly disappear. It was thought by the contractors that the cylinder, having penetrated over 40 feet of sand, had encountered a layer of swamp which had swallowed it up, but when the weather allowed the divers to investigate it was found that the top of the caisson had been snapped clean off by the waves at the level of the concrete filling. With it had gone the pumping and air compressing machinery and the boiler that powered it. Thus ended the first attempt to erect a lighthouse on the Rothersand shoal and with it the short life of the company.

In the following March the Harkoort Company were asked if they were still willing to undertake the work. The company was now in a very strong position and it demanded—and obtained—the sum of £42,650 to build the lighthouse and to equip it with all but the lighting apparatus. The general building plan was the same as that used by the earlier company but with several important modifications. The new engineers designed an oval-shaped caisson 46 feet long, 36 feet wide and 61 feet high when launched; the height was increased during the sinking to 107 feet. Made of half-inch thick boiler iron, the caisson was braced vertically and horizontally. Eight feet above the cutting edge was an iron floor forming the top of the working chamber through which rose the air shaft with its air-lock. The upper part of the caisson was divided into four floors. The first for mixing the concrete; the second containing the boilers and machinery; the third forming the living and sleeping quarters for the men; while the top storey carried two cranes. As the caisson sank into the sand and its walls increased in height, the floors would, of course, have to be raised as the lower part was filled with concrete, and this raising was effected by suspending the floors from long screws. By this method all the floors, together with what was on them, could be raised without stopping the work.

The completed caisson, together with its equipment and ballast, weighed some 600 tons, and the towing operation proved to be a hazardous one. The towing cables, 5 inches in diameter, were specially made for the job and the two strongest tugs owned by North German Lloyd were chartered in addition to three other tugs. It was realized that the operation could only be carried out in the calmest of weather and at ebb tide, so the task force of eighty men and five steamers waited for the go-ahead from the weather station. For fifty-five days they waited with the ship's fires banked and steam raised with every man prepared to go into action at a moment's notice. On the evening of 15 May the weather stations sent word that the tow could be attempted, and at 3.30 a.m. on the following day the caisson, which now resembled a floating factory, moved out of the basin, accompanied by the entire fleet of nine vessels engaged in the constructional work. At 7.15 a.m., as the tide turned, the whole procession dropped anchor to await the next high water at 4 p.m. The flood current, however, was much stronger than had been anticipated and at 11 o'clock in the morning the caisson, dragging and straining at the two tugs holding her, caused them to slip their anchors.

Hurriedly the tugs attempted to get under way but they found they could not hold the iron mass which, in fact, began to tow them backwards. Two more tugs came to their help, and under the combined effort of 350 horse-power the caisson was held until the tide diminished. When the fleet reached Hoheweg lighthouse a signal was received from the keepers that severe squalls were approaching the area. The flotilla at once came to anchor and everything was made ready for the approaching storm which burst on them with great violence at five in the afternoon. However, the caisson rode it out very well and no damage was done. The weather continuing bad throughout the night and the following day, it was not until the morning of the third day that the voyage was continued. At 11 a.m. the caisson was on site. The valves were opened and the iron barrel sank slowly, steadily and in perfect plumb to the ocean's bed. The remainder of the season was spent in burying it in the sand as quickly as possible in order that it should be firmly secure against the winter's storms. Working under compressed air in the space between the bottom floor and the sea-bed, the men excavated the sand, thus forcing the cutting edge deeper and deeper, while metal workers heightened the outside walls of the cylinder correspondingly. In the meantime, concrete was mixed and poured into the ever-increasing area above the working chamber and under this extra weight the sinking process was made easier and faster. By the middle of October the walls of the cylinder were 100 feet above the cutting edge which by now was buried to a depth of 51 feet below low water. At this point work was stopped for the winter and the caisson was left in the charge of two keepers.

After a winter of particularly violent storms which left the caisson unscathed, work recommenced in February 1884. By May the caisson had been sunk to its required depth of 73 feet below low water and the concrete filling had reached a height of 3 feet above low water. In June the machinery and boilers were removed and the stone masons started work. By November the solid base of the tower, the cellar, the store-rooms and kitchen were finished and the outside wall of the living-room was built. By August 1885 the lighthouse was complete. The lantern-room is 80 feet above low-water level and rises from a base 33 feet in diameter. The tower has an unusual appearance for a wave-swept lighthouse, there being three medieval-like turrets near the top with dormer windows accommodating secondary lights.

Subsequent inspection of the submarine foundation of the lighthouse revealed a considerable erosion of the sea-bed caused by the race of the tide. To check this, 175,000 cubic feet of brushwood were sunk around the tower and 600 tons of stone were lowered to keep it in place.

I I

Fin de Siècle

IT WAS ANNOUNCED in 1877 that Smeaton's historic lighthouse on Eddystone Rock was to be demolished and replaced by a new one. The persistent sea had destroyed much of the cement at the base of the tower and, worse, it had undermined that part of the rock on which the tower stood. At first it was proposed to blow up the reef, thus removing the need for a light altogether, but when this scheme was examined it was calculated that two million tons of rock would have to be blasted and the cost of the operation would be ten times that of building a new tower.

The engineer-in-chief of Trinity House in 1877 was James Nicholas Douglass, who had gained his experience in lighthouse building on Wolf and Bishop's Rocks which, together with Eddystone are considered the three most hazardous building sites on the English coast. It was fitting therefore that to James Douglass should fall the task of putting a fourth tower on Eddystone. Douglass had recently completed an extraordinary repair job on the tower that he and his father had built in 1851–8 on Bishop's Rock; magnificent though it was, this tower had proved neither tall nor mighty enough to withstand the terrible violence of the sea at that place. On one occasion in 1860 a bell weighing three hundredweight was plucked from its lashings 120 feet up on the gallery and hurled onto the rocks where it smashed to pieces. After twenty years of such violation the tower began to yield and during very heavy weather it would shake like a leaf to the understandable concern of its keepers. Finally, ominous cracks appeared in the granite blocks from which the tower was constructed and James Douglass was called in to see what could be done. As a temporary measure he strengthened the building by fixing iron ties to the inner walls, but his plans for permanently strengthening the fabric were daring. Douglass proposed to build a new tower around the old one and to make a homogeneous whole by dovetailing the outer tower into the existing inner one. First the foundations were increased to a diameter of 40 feet, with massive granite blocks sunk, cemented and bolted into the rock. Further blocks were built upwards, each one dovetailed not only to the one below and the one either side but also to the stones of the original building. The task of cutting the dovetailing in the old tower was a dangerous one as the men engaged in it worked from a platform suspended from the lighthouse gallery. Life-lines were also hung from the gallery and a man was provided to watch the sea. When he saw a big wave coming he blew a whistle and the men perched high up on the lighthouse wall stopped work on the instant to hang onto the lines for their lives. Four extra floors were added to the top of the tower, making its total height above sea-level 163 feet.

Douglass's design for a new Eddystone lighthouse was based on Smeaton's with the difference that the new tower was to be 136 feet high—or nearly twice the height of the old one. Another important difference was that instead of tapering up from its base the new tower was to be built on a solid cylinder of masonry 22 feet in height and 44 feet in diameter. The first 23 feet of the tower proper were also to be solid and above this there would be nine storeys compared to Smeaton's four.

The site selected for the new tower was about 120 feet from the old one and was situated at a lower level. This considerably lessened the length of the early working periods, but as Douglass had steam-boats at his command he was able to work much longer seasons. Operations started in July 1878 and five months were worked in this first season. The first job was, of course, the inevitably dreary and backbreaking one of hewing a level foundation out of the obdurate gneiss of Eddystone and sinking a circular coffer-dam into the rock. All the foundation stones were dovetailed, not only to each other, but into the reef as well. Much of this work was carried out by men waist deep in water, secured by ropes to boats standing by in case they were swept into the sea. The coffer-dam took nearly a year to build and was pumped dry in June 1879. By the spring of 1880 the top of the completed granite base rose 30 inches above high-water level; it was then possible to work throughout the year. The 2,171 granite blocks used for the tower weighed on average $2\frac{1}{2}$ tons apiece, each being dovetailed to its neighbours on five of its six surfaces (see Plate 3a). On 18 May 1882 the lamp was lit by the Duke of Edinburgh, then Master of Trinity House. The lighting apparatus was of the Fresnel dioptric type of 79,250 candle power, giving a double flash, while, in a lower room, two other lamps threw a fixed beam onto the dangerous Hands Deep Rock, some three and a half miles away to the north-west. The lamp was converted to electricity in 1959 and now produces 570,000 candle power—a far cry indeed from Smeaton's tallow candles.

Douglass had estimated that the tower would take five years to build and that it would cost £78,000. In the result the work was completed in three and a half years at a cost of £59,250. A few weeks after the light was first lit Douglass received a knighthood from Queen Victoria 'on the occasion of the completion of the new Eddystone lighthouse, with which your name is so honourably connected'.

Douglass's tower did not mean the end of Smeaton's historic building. Regarded as a national monument, the upper half was re-erected on Plymouth Hoe where, within its lantern-room, Smeaton's original candelabra can still be seen. The lower half, filled with masonry and bevelled off at the top, still neighbours its successor on the Eddystone (see Plate 3b).

The year 1890 saw the invention of an improved method for rotating lights. The light carriage in the first revolving lights was mounted on rollers running on a race path, the resulting friction limiting the speed of rotation and consequently the size and power of the light. The new idea was to float the optical apparatus in a bath of mercury, thus practically eliminating all friction and allowing it to rotate at a relatively high speed. Apparatus weighing five tons or more can, mounted by this method, be moved around with one finger. The older optics revolved at about once every four minutes, but the introduction of the mercury bath made revolutions of fifteen to twenty seconds possible. Seeing that the duration of a flash is decreased as the speed of rotation increases, group flashing became desirable. Instead of a single flash followed by a relatively long period of darkness, a number of flashes—between two and five—were introduced, given in quick succession and followed by a longer dark period. This, of course, greatly helps the navigator to take bearings.

Five miles out to sea from Cape Clear the Fastnet tower springs from its rocky bed like a great tree (see Plate 8a). This, the most famous of all Irish beacons, is the first and last light seen by transatlantic voyagers, and because of its associations with the Irish emigrant it has acquired the horribly sentimental name of 'the tear drop of Ireland'.

An earlier lighthouse on Fastnet, completed in 1854 by George Halpin, took six years to build. Placed on the very summit of the rock, it was a cast-iron structure, 63 feet 9 inches high by 19 feet 6 inches in diameter. The lantern, some 170 feet above low-water level, was a dioptric type of 38,000 candle power. The keepers lived in a separate house on the north-east side of the rock. Even at the height at which it was placed, the tower was subject to the hammering of storm waves, and after a while the keepers complained that during bad weather it shook appreciably. On one occasion a piece of rock weighing three tons was snatched from the rock cliff by one wave and hurled back at the tower with the next. After ten years of this sort of treatment it became clear that the lighthouse would not survive unless something was done to strengthen it considerably.

An external casing was built around the base of the tower extending to the second floor, the annular space between this and the original wall being filled with stones. Then, any projecting pieces of the rock were removed and hollows filled with concrete so as to lessen resistance to the waves. The two bottom storeys of the tower were filled in, the keepers' house abandoned and the upper rooms of the lighthouse furnished as dwellings. This reinforced tower stood up well enough, but after a sea had reached up to the lantern itself, breaking the outside glass and damaging a lens, it was decided to replace it. At the time another member of the Douglass family was engineer to the Commissioners of Irish Lights. This was William Douglass, and his recommendation was to ignore the advantage to be gained in building on top of the rock and to base a granite column on a hard, solid ledge of rock 6 inches below high-water level. It was to be 176 feet high with a base diameter of 52 feet.

In August 1896 work began on the rock under the foremanship of James Kavanagh, a skilled mason, who, during the four years of dangerous, backbreaking toil that it took to complete the tower, hardly ever left the site. First a boiler and steam winch were installed on the ledge to land the men and materials, and then the hard rock was attacked to prepare a foundation for the first course of masonry. This work was carried out under the most uncomfortable and perilous conditions, for every big breaker submerged the site completely and would have swept away any man who had not grabbed a life-line.

Because of the continuous swell it was not possible for the supply boat to draw up to the rock—men and materials were landed and embarked by a rope suspended between the rock and the tender. The stone blocks were of the finest Cornish granite weighing between four and five tons apiece. Each one was dressed and dovetailed ashore, packed into a wooden crate to protect its edges, and put onto the tender. The blocks were too heavy to be swung ashore on the rope, so they were landed by a most ingenious method. A derrick was erected on the rock with a long boom which could be swung out towards the tender. A rope from the end of the boom was attached to the crated granite block which was then gently lowered into the water. The derrick's topping-lift was then hauled in, bringing the submerged stone to the foot of the tower where it was lifted ashore. Two thousand and seventy-four stones, weighing 4,633 tons, were landed in this way.

Life on the rock was arduous to say the least and the men seldom went ashore at less than three-month intervals. Each man was compelled to supply and cook his own food and Kavanagh maintained the strictest discipline. In addition to his duties as foreman, he acted as medical inspector and welfare officer, only leaving the rock during the short periods when the weather made work impossible. On two occasions he remained on Fastnet for the entire year.

The tower was completed in June 1903 and the job of installing the lantern was immediately started. The apparatus, landed safely, was carried up the rock for a distance where it was stored. That very night a particularly savage storm descended on Fastnet, enveloping the rock with heavy waves. In the morning it was found that most of the lantern parts had completely disappeared, while those that remained were badly damaged. There now being no possibility of completing the light for many months, the lantern of the old tower was transferred to the new, where it shone for another year. In the following summer the new lantern was safely installed. It was the first of a type that was to become standard in oil-burning lighthouses. The oil was vaporized under pressure and the resulting gas was fed to Bunsen burners giving a light of 1,200 candle power, which, intensified through dioptric lenses, gave 750,000 candle power. The old tower was used as an oil-store. The new light was first shown in July 1904.

Sad to relate, James Kavanagh never saw the new Fastnet light which his energies had done so much towards establishing. Having lived on the rock almost continuously for nearly seven years he went ashore after the last masonry course was laid complaining of feeling ill. He died of a stroke a few days before the new light was lit.

Sir Robert Ball, scientific adviser to the Commissioners of Irish Lights, sailed out from Crookhaven on the night of 21 July 1904 to inspect the new Fastnet light:

As to the beams of the Fastnet during all the time of our return to harbour, I cannot describe them other than by saying they were magnificent. At ten miles' distance the great revolving spokes of light, succeeding each other at intervals of five seconds, gave the most distinctive character possible. Almost before one spoke had disappeared the next came into view, but the effect was doubtless in part attributable to the haze. It was a most beautiful optical phenomenon. Each great flash, as it swept past, lighted up the ship and the rigging like a search-light.

There is a touch of *fin de siècle* about the noble tower that rises from the foot of the chalk cliffs of Beachy Head for it was one of the last of the classic granite towers to be built off the coast of Britain. This Sussex headland was previously lit by a beacon placed on the crown of the cliff but it was found that the light was frequently obscured by the mists that rise around Beachy Head. A new tower became a matter of urgency when it was discovered that the constant battering of the sea had undermined the site of the old light. The designer of the new lighthouse was Sir Thomas Mathews and he described his gracefully curving tower as a 'concave, elliptic frustrum'.

Investigations showed the sea-bed at the foot of the cliffs to be of hard chalk, dense enough to make an ideal foundation, and a site was chosen some 550 feet off the shore. As the water on the site was very deep at high tide a coffer-dam was built that could be pumped dry at low water; within this a circular excavation was made to a depth of 10 feet to take the first granite courses. Blasting could not be resorted to in making the hole for fear of splitting the chalk foundation, so the early work was carried out with picks and shovels. It is surprising that pneumatic power tools were not used, but Messrs Bullivant and Company, the builders, must have had their reasons. Beside the site a tall landing platform was built which was connected to the top of the cliffs by a cableway comprising two 6-inch diameter ropes in a parallel span of 600 feet with a combined breaking strain of 220 tons (see Plate 7). All the men, tools and materials were carried out to the works by this means including 3,660 tons of granite blocks already dressed and dovetailed. The 153-foot-high tower, finished in 1902, springs from a base 47 feet in diameter.

12

Towers of the New World

THE AMERICAS' FIRST lighthouse was lit in September 1716, an event which was announced by this news item in the *Boston News Letter*:

Boston. By virtue of an Act of Assembly made in the First Year of His Majesty's Reign, For Building and Maintaining a Light House upon the Great Brewster (called Beacon-Island) at the Entrance of the Harbour of Boston, in order to prevent the loss of the Lives and Estates of His Majesty's Subjects; The said Light House has been built; and on Fryday last the 14th Currant the Light was kindled, which will be very useful for all Vessels going out and coming in to the Harbour of Boston, or any other Harbours in the Massachusetts Bay, for which all Masters shall pay to the Receiver of Impost, one Penny per Ton Inwards, and another Penny Outwards, except Coasters, who are to pay Two Shillings each, at their clearance Out, And all Fishing Vessels, Wood Sloops, etc. Five Shillings each by the Year.

Boston lighthouse was a stone cone-shaped tower illuminated by tallow candles which were later superseded by an oil-lamp. The first keeper was one George Worthylake, husbandman, who received a salary of £50 a year which later rose to £70 because, says the record, 'he lost 59 sheep by drowning in a severe storm, his attendance on the Light House preventing him from saving them'. In November 1718 Worthylake, his wife, daughter and Negro slave were all drowned when, while on a trip to Noddle's Island, their boat capsized.

In 1761 a lottery was organized in New York to raise the money to build a much-needed lighthouse in the harbour, but only £26 was realized. The following year a more successful lottery raised enough money to build a nine-storeyed, 85-foot-high tower at Sandy Hook which was described by the newspapers as the best light on the continent. At the time only three others existed. The keeper's contract of service allowed him the 'privilege of keeping and pasturing two cows' but also stipulated that he should not use the tower as a 'public-house for selling strong liquors'.

Lighthouses in the United States were administered by local coastal authorities until the year 1789 when the Federal Government assumed charge and created a Lighthouse Establishment which took control of the twelve light-stations then existing around the seaboard of the United States; these were Boston, Brant Point, Beaver Tail, New London, Sandy Hook, Cape Henlopen, Charleston, Gurnet, Portsmouth, Cape Ann, Great Point and Newburyport.

George Washington took a particular and personal interest in lighthouse affairs and many documents relating to them bear his signature. One of his first actions on becoming president was to write a letter to the keeper of Sandy Hook light instructing him to keep his light burning until such time as Congress could provide funds for its maintenance.

Another lighthouse enthusiast was President Jefferson who wrote many letters on the subject. His endorsement on a letter written to him in 1808 asking for his approval of the appointment of one Jared Hand as keeper of the Montauk light in succession to his father, reads: 'I have constantly refused to give in to this method of making offices hereditary. Whenever this one becomes actually vacant, the claims of Jared Hand may be considered with those of other competitors.' Elsewhere we learn from Jefferson's writings that 'the keepers of lighthouses should be dismissed for small degrees of remissness, because of the calamities which even these produce'.

When the responsibility for building lighthouses was assumed by the Federal Government the growth in their number was rapid. The twelve establishments taken over in 1789 had, by 1800, become twenty-four. In 1820 there were fifty-five and by 1852 the department administered no fewer than 325 lights around the coasts of the United States. The lighthouses were maintained by private contractors who, in return for a fixed annual sum, were bound to keep the buildings in a good state of repair, supply oil and all other stores and to pay the keepers.

The general efficiency of this system can be judged from the following report of an inspector after a visit to Sandy Hook lighthouse in 1852:

The tower of Sandy Hook main light was constructed in 1764, under royal charter, of rubble stone, and is now in a good state of preservation. The inside walls of the tower had been recently whitewashed but two years had elapsed since the outside had been done. The keeper is not instructed in the manner of adjusting the apparatus and had entered upon his duties without any previous instruction. . . . The fact that there is only one keeper at Sandy Hook, while there are five at Navesink, cannot fail to be remarked upon. . . . The lights are not lighted at sunsetting, and kept burning until sunrise, in compliance with instructions. The keeper uses his own discretion in this matter, generally lighting about dusk and extinguishing at daylight.

The keeper stated that the oil last year was bad; the winter oil was cut, in cold weather, with a knife. The Sandy Hook lights are not trimmed during the night; in the keeper's opinion they do not require it!

Twenty-five miles out in the North Atlantic ocean, in the direct path of a busy sea-way, lies the huge mass of Matinicus Rock. Exposing an area of 39 acres at low tide, this jagged reef is a dreadful hazard to ships at night or in unfavourable weather. The first lighthouse on this desolate island, consisting of a stone living-house with a wooden light tower at each end, was built in 1827. A new, more substantial building was put there in 1846, following the lines of the old one but constructed entirely of granite. The original buildings were left in place and used as store-houses.

The keeper of the Matinicus light during the years 1853 to 1861 was Samuel Burgess, who lived on the rock with his invalid wife and four daughters. The eldest of the girls, Abbie, was fourteen when she first came to Matinicus, and in addition to looking after the family she also performed the duties of assistant keeper, sometimes caring for the light for days on end when her father was ashore. It was during one of his absences that Matinicus Rock was assailed by a storm of almost unprece-dented fury—the same storm which, as we shall see, completely obliterated the near-by Minot's Ledge lighthouse and its keepers. There can be no doubt that the steadfastness of Abbie Burgess was the inspiration for many of the Victorian romances that were written on the theme of the lighthouse-keeper's daughter. The incident is best described by Abbie Burgess her-self in a letter she wrote to a friend:

You have often expressed a desire to view the sea out upon the ocean when it is angry. Had you been here on the 19 of January, I surmise you would have been satisfied. Father was away. Early in the day, as the tide arose, the sea made a complete breach over the rock, washing every movable thing away, and of the old dwelling not one stone was left upon another. The new dwelling was flooded, and the windows had to be secured to prevent the violence of the spray from breaking them in. As the tide came, the sea rose higher and higher, till the only endurable places were the light-towers. If they stood we were saved, otherwise our fate was all too certain. . . . *For four weeks*, owing to rough weather, no land-ing could be effected on the rock. . . . Though at times greatly exhausted with my labors, not once did the lights fail. Under God I was able to perform all my accustomed duties as well as my father's.

You know the hens were our only companions. Becoming convinced, as the gale increased, that unless they were brought into the house they would be lost . . . I ran out a few yards after the rollers had passed and the sea fell off a little, with the water knee deep, to the coop and rescued all but one. It was the work of a moment, and I was back in the house with the door fastened, but I was none too quick, for at that instant my little sister, standing at the window, exclaimed: 'Oh, look! look there! the worst sea is coming!' That wave destroyed the old dwelling and swept the rock. I cannot think you would enjoy remaining here any great length of time for the sea is never still, and when agitated, its roar shuts out every other sound, even drowning our voices.

On another occasion, when the weather prevented the visit of the supply boat, provisions on the rock were so reduced that Burgess risked the trip to the mainland himself in a small boat. It was three weeks before he was able to return and during that time the mother and the four girls subsisted on one egg and a cup of corn-meal a day and again Abbie maintained the light as well as looking after the family.

In 1861 Burgess found other employment and left his daughter on the rock to instruct his successor, a Captain Grant. Grant had a son, so it is not surprising that upon that lonely rock romance flourished. Captain Grant's son, Isaac, married Abbie Burgess that same year, and fourteen years later Abbie, now the mother of four children, was still on Matinicus Rock. In 1875 Isaac Grant was appointed keeper of White Head Light with his wife as assistant.

The most famous of all American lighthouses, Minot's Ledge, is one of the finest in the world and ranks as one of the great achievements in marine engineering. A report calling for a light at this dreadful spot described the ledge as 'annually the scene of the most heart-rending disasters . . . causing the death of many a brave seaman and the loss of large amounts of property. Not a winter passes without one or more of these fearful disasters occurring.' In the space of nine years, 1832 to 1841, no fewer than forty vessels were wrecked on Minot's Ledge and its surrounding reefs and from six of them there were no survivors. The area was well described by Captain W. H. Swift who erected the first beacon there.

Minot's Rocks—or as they are more generally called 'The Minot's'—lie off the south-eastern chop of Boston Bay. These rocks or ledges, with others in their immediate vicinity, are also known as the 'Cohasset Rocks', and have been the terror of mariners for a long period of years; they have been, probably, the cause of a greater number of wrecks than any other ledges or reefs upon the coast. The Minot's are bare only at three-quarters ebb, and vessels bound in with the wind heavy at north-east, are liable, if they fall to the leeward of Boston light, to be driven upon these reefs.

'Outer Minot', the most seaward of the group, was selected as the site for the lighthouse. Consisting of hard granite, the rock is 3½ feet above extreme low water at which times an area of about 30 feet in diameter is exposed. It is unusual, however, for more than a 25 feet diameter to be left bare by the sea.

Captain Swift began building the first beacon in 1847 and the work occupied two seasons. With the water constantly breaking over the meagre surface available, the work of drilling had to be done by machinery raised well out of the reach of the sea and even then the working periods were short as the rock could only be reached during the calmest spells of weather.

Swift had decided on an iron skeleton structure as offering the least resistance to the waves. The form of the lighthouse was octagonal, 25 feet in diameter at its base, and, like the Maplin Sands light, the structure was supported on 9-inch diameter wrought-iron piles—eight situated at the angles of the octagon and one in the centre. Holes were driven 5 feet deep into the rock to receive the piles, those for the outer ones being driven at an inclination that brought their heads within a circle of 14 feet diameter; on the top they were keyed and bolted to a heavy iron casting which formed the platform for the lighthouse. The work was finished in November 1848 and for the first time a light shone to warn navigators of the menace of the Minot's. The living accommodation was provided by a small iron house beneath the lantern in which, for three years, two men lived with the continual din of pounding waves. The three years ended, as will be seen, by a tragedy caused by the keepers themselves.

On 14 April 1851 a severe storm broke over the coast of Massachusetts which by the next day had developed into a violent gale. By the morning of Wednesday the 16th the gale had become a hurricane of such violence that the lighthouse was surrounded and sometimes completely enveloped in the moving mountains of water. It was, of course, impossible to reach the keepers in their peril and when dusk fell that night many eyes were turned towards Minot's Ledge for the sight of the light that would show that the keepers were still alive. The light appeared at its usual time although from the shore it could only be observed intermittently because of the huge waves that obscured the tower from view. Then, at 10 o'clock, the light went out and instead could be heard the sonorous tolling of the lighthouse bell. It was deduced later that the poor keepers, their refuge heeling into the surf and slowly breaking up, were vainly signalling for help from the shore. Half an hour later, on the turn of the tide, when from the opposition of wind and current the sea was at its highest mark, the bell stopped its chiming and was not heard again. At daylight the sea went down a little and Minot's Ledge could be seen from the shore. The lighthouse had completely vanished—all that remained being a few bent piles projecting from the rock. The cause of the disaster was explained by Captain Swift. Referring to a series of horizontal braces placed between the piles some 38 feet above the rock, he wrote:

Upon these braces the keeper had improperly built a sort of deck or platform, upon which were placed heavy articles such as fuel, water-barrels, etc., which should have been in the store-room designed for their reception. The deck, in addition to the weight placed upon it, was fastened together and secured to the piles and braces, thus offering a large surface, against which the sea could strike. In addition to this, the keeper had attached a five-and-a-half inch hawser to the lantern deck, and anchored the other end to a granite block, weighing, according to his account, seven tons, placed upon the bottom at a distance of some fifty fathoms from the base of the tower. The object of this was to provide a means for running a box or landing-chair up and down; but it is very clear that so much surface exposed to the moving sea had the same effect upon the lighthouse as would have been produced by a number of men pulling at a rope attached to the highest part of the structure, with the *design* of pulling it down.

Part of the structure was later recovered and its examination by engineers confirmed Captain Swift's theory. The bodies of the unfortunate keepers were never found.

Although the first light on Minot's had been disastrously beaten by the sea, the dramatic decrease in the number of shipwrecks in the area during its short life had demonstrated the absolute necessity of its presence, with the result that after the disaster Congress lost no time in making money available to erect a more massive building to house a new light. Because of the sensational nature of the accident the newly formed United States Lighthouse Board were, understandably, apprehensive of making another effort to build on the Minot's, and it was not until 1855 that the problem was again tackled.

The new lighthouse, designed by General G. J. Totten, a member of the Board, was to be a granite tower 102 feet high. Captain B. S. Alexander, a military engineer of great experience, was given the task of building it. Alexander made his first visit to Minot's Ledge on 1 May 1855 and after a survey he came to the following conclusions which he embodied in a report to the Lighthouse Board on 31 May. Even in summer, landing would be impossible for weeks on end; the greater part of the ledge was continually submerged and the rest only above the surface for three to four hours a day; the space was extremely confined; during easterly weather the sea broke over the rock with such violence that it would be impossible to build a coffer-dam. The cutting of the rock foundations would be a long, hazardous and costly operation, requiring incessant vigilance and the employment of a large number of skilled men. That to engage such a party and place them on vessels near the rock would mean that the men would be idle nine-tenths of the time and in consequence discipline would become lax and the men unused to work. It was therefore proposed to combine the operation of hewing out the rock foundation with that of preparing the masonry, thus ensuring the men full employment and wages. The men would work in a shore establishment, cutting, shaping and dressing the granite blocks and, when weather permitted, a gang of them would be sent out to work on the ledge.

This admirable scheme was accepted and on 1 July 1855 (a Sunday) a small party landed on the rock and started cutting the foundations. While this work was in progress the rest of the task-force was engaged in building an iron scaffold on the ledge to be used as a derrick for laying the lower courses of masonry and as a refuge for the men in case of sudden tempest. This scaffold was built into the nine holes that had secured the first lighthouse. As soon as new piles had been fixed into these holes a network of life-lines was laid between them to afford handholds for the men against the breakers that regularly submerged the working surface.

The first two seasons, during which only 134 and 157 hours respectively could be worked, were devoted to the levelling of the granite and to the building of the scaffold; and it was not until 1857 that the first blocks of masonry were laid. As the greater part of the site was under water, extreme difficulty was met with in the laying of the first course, but this was overcome by a most ingenious method. Small 'coffer-dams' were built from sandbags around the site of each block of stone. These bags, being pliable, adapted to the contours of the rock thus allowing the water within them to be sponged out. When the area was perfectly dry it was covered with a layer of cement upon which was laid a sheet of muslin which protected the cement from any incoming water. Previous experiments had shown that the cement would penetrate the muslin and make a good bond to the first course of stone.

During 1858, 208 hours were worked and the masonry was carried up to the sixth course. The following year saw the completion of the thirty-second course at the cost of 337 hours of toil and, in 1860, after five years' work, the tower was completed. Because of the limited space available for the base the tower is purely conical and lacks the tree-like spread at the base which was usual for lighthouses of that period. Each of the 1,079 stones used in the tower was secured to its neighbours by heavy iron dogs while the first twelve courses were additionally strengthened by means of stout iron rods passing through them and into the holes in the rock that had been sunk by Captain Swift. The overall height of Minot's Ledge tower is 102 feet and it contains 5,881 tons of granite. The light was first shown in November 1860 and has shown its warning ray ever since (see Plate 4). In 1947 Minot's Ledge lighthouse, a lonely home for generations of keepers, was made automatic.

The American lighthouse service was much involved in the Civil War. Nearly all the lighthouses on the southern coasts, one-third of all United States lights, were seized by the Confederate army and many lightships captured and sunk as a means of obstructing channels. In July 1863 the lighthouse tender *Martha* was taken and burned while the tenders at Charleston and Mobile were captured and put to warlike uses. As soon as possible after the war the lighthouse service on the southern coasts was fully restored.

13

The Nineteenth Century in America

THE GREAT LAKES of North America, the largest areas of fresh water in the world, are subject to storms and tempests that are worthy of the Atlantic Ocean. Additionally, they are subject to dense fog and the even worse menace of ice. The shores of these inland seas are as tortuous and treacherous as some of the worst on ocean seaboards, and as they are regularly navigated by freighters the need for adequate lighting is essential.

At the northern end of Lake Huron, off the Straits of Mackinac, there lie two submerged reefs of limestone rock littered with boulders which seen from above resemble a giant pair of spectacles. On a rock at the northerly end of the range stands Spectacle Reef lighthouse, the Eddystone of the Great Lakes. The immense strength of this tower is required not to withstand the force of the water, considerable though that is, but rather to resist the ice that forms in the winter months. Ice formed from fresh water is extremely hard and when moved by currents is almost irresistible. Lighthouses built on the Lakes, therefore, are designed not so much to resist the intermittent poundings of waves but to withstand a continuous pressure from thousands of tons of solid, piling ice.

Spectacle Reef took a regular toll of shipping from the time the Great Lakes were navigated but it was not until 1867, when two large ships were simultaneously torn to pieces on its hidden spurs, that the building of a lighthouse became a matter of great urgency.

The first detailed survey of the reef was carried out in 1868 when it was found that the least depth of water was 7 feet while the most suitable site for a lighthouse was found at a depth of 11 feet. General O. M. Poe, the engineer selected to build the light was, like the builder of Minot's Ledge, a military engineer, and he decided to use Minot's tower as his model. His plan was to first build a 'protection pier' which was in fact to be a square wooden coffer-dam enclosing some 50 square feet into which was to be placed a second, circular, coffer-dam in which the men were to work on the foundations. The protection pier comprised a square box, 12 feet high, divided into a series of vertical compartments on all four sides. The pier was built at Scammon's Harbour during 1870–71, then towed to its site. Here it was sunk by filling the outer compartments with ballast stone, the compartments being decked over to make a pier. A schooner having been moored to this pier to accommodate the workmen, the task of sinking the coffer-dam proper was started. This coffer-dam was required to rest on a very uneven rocky bed—a difficulty which was overcome as follows. The cylinder forming the inner coffer-dam was made up of wooden staves, each 15 feet long, braced and trussed internally and held together on the outside by hoops of iron so that it resembled a barrel some 36 feet wide. It was assembled above the surface of the water and, when completed, thick, twisted oakum was fastened around the lower edge; outside this was fixed a thicker rope made of twisted hay. The completed coffer-dam was lowered carefully onto the reef until the highest projection was reached. Then each stave of the cylinder was driven down separately until it reached the rock, the oakum and hay being driven down likewise and acting as caulking between the staves and the rock. In this way a waterproof joint was formed between the lower edge of the coffer-dam and the uneven contours of the rock. With the inner coffer-dam securely in position, powerful pumps were set to work to empty it of water, leaving the inside dry for the men to start work.

The reef was cleaned off and levelled and the first course of granite was bolted home. Each stone was secured to all its neighbours by wrought-iron bolts, 2 feet long and $2\frac{1}{2}$ inches thick. Liquid cement was forced under pressure into all the bolt holes and joints between the stones so that the result was a near monolith and as one with the rock beneath it. It should not be thought that a summer season on Lake Huron resembles one on the Norfolk Broads and the following account of a storm at Spectacle Reef will give some idea of conditions there:

The sea burst in the doors and windows of the workmen's quarters, tore up the floors and all the bunks on the side nearest the edge of the pier and the platform between the quarters and the pier. Everything in the quarters was completely demolished except the kitchen which remained serviceable. . . . Several timbers on the east side of the crib were driven in some four inches, and the temporary cribs were completely swept away. The north side was so completely filled up that the steamer can no longer lie there. A stone weighing thirty pounds was thrown across the pier; but the greatest feat accomplished by the gale was the moving of the revolving derrick from the northeast to the southwest corner.

At three o'clock in the morning the men were obliged to run for their lives, and the only shelter they found was on the west side of the tower. The sea finally moderated sufficiently to allow them to seek refuge in the small cement shanty standing near the southeast corner of the crib.

The building of Spectacle Reef tower was started in May 1870 and completed in June 1874 and during the whole four years the total working period was about twenty months. The tower is a frustrum of a cone rising from a base of 32 feet diameter to a height of 93 feet.

Turning from the Great Lakes to the Atlantic seaboard, the coasts of Florida are exposed to particularly severe gales. The numerous reefs in the vicinity are mainly lighted by screw-pile lighthouses, the most notable of which is the one situated on Fowey Rocks. Built in 1876, this lighthouse is in the form of an octagonal pyramid containing two decks—the lower one housing the keepers and the upper one the light, which is 110 feet above high water (an illustration of a lighthouse similar to this will be found on Plate 5a). At low water the surface of the reef is only 3 feet down and the first operation was the building of a wooden platform on this surface. The platform, 80 feet square by 12 feet high, was supported by piles driven 10 feet into the rock. Great care was necessary to ensure that the piles were absolutely vertical. A disc was lowered onto the rock and put into position for the central pile; then, through a hole in the centre of this disc, the first iron pile was driven home. After each single blow of the pile-driver the pile was tested with a plumbline, the slightest deviation from the vertical being corrected by tackles. When the central pile was secured in the rock a gauge, consisting of a heavy iron beam, was lowered to the bottom with one end in contact with the edge of the disc. The first of the perimeter discs was then positioned to touch the other end of the beam and a pile driven through it. After that two gauges were used—one to maintain the proper distance from the centre pile and the other to measure the distance from the perimeter pile previously driven. When all the piles were in position, the tops were levelled off and sockets attached to them. Horizontal girders and diagonal tie-rods were attached and the first deck was put into place. Until the keepers' living-quarters were built the men were accommodated in tents erected on the platform and life in that improvised camp some four miles out at sea was alarming as well as uncomfortable. A hurricane, if it came, would have carried away not only the tents but the men themselves, and with any sort of a sea running the waves hammered at the wooden platform making it quiver. When the first deck and the keepers' quarters were completed, progress on the superstructure was rapid and in June 1878 the light was shown.

Eight miles from New London, Connecticut, lies a very dangerous submerged reef known, because of the high velocity of the tides that sweep it, as Race Rock. Its peak is never less than 3 feet below low water and, as the area is subject to dense fogs and heavy ice as well as the force of the Atlantic, Race Rock is a veritable graveyard of shipping. During the eight years immediately preceding the building of a lighthouse, eight large ships, as well as many smaller ones, were wrecked on this reef.

The decision to build a lighthouse was made in 1872. F. Hopkinson Smith, then better known as an artist than as a lighthouse builder, was appointed engineer-in-chief with Captain Thomas Scott as his resident engineer. The latter was a most fortunate choice for Scott proved himself to be a man of tenacity, energy and resourcefulness—qualities that are demanded of the engineer at the best of times, but which in the case of Race Rock lighthouse were to be in constant demand during the seven years it took to complete the work.

The rock marks the south-western point of Ram Island, between Long Island Sound and Ram Island Sound. The speed of the notorious current that races through its crags is some 6 m.p.h., and the nearest supply point is eight miles away. These, then, were the conditions that faced the engineers in 1872—conditions which would have made the sinking of a caisson a very hazardous operation indeed. It was decided instead to raise the surface of the reef above sea-level by building it up with stones. Thousands of rocks, weighing up to 7 tons each, were brought out to the site by barges and heaved overboard. This work went on for over a year until, at last, an artificial island of over 60 feet in diameter was visible at low water. The next step was to level off this island in preparation for the first granite course. If the word 'delicacy' can be applied to the operation of blasting hard rock it is appropriate here; each boulder was drilled in several carefully selected places and precise charges of powder were so skilfully situated that when they were detonated they produced a level surface. There being no shelter on the tiny 'island', extra long fuses were used; when these were lit the working party hurried into a boat which, with the help of the famous current, enabled them to reach a safe distance before the explosion occurred. When the current was at its strongest it took a considerable time and much energy to row back to the works, so the resourceful Scott had a deep pit blasted in the centre of the islet which, being roofed over, served as a shelter for the men; it was always at least half full of water and with a rising tide the men were submerged up to their necks.

After many months of toil and mishaps, which included the deaths of three men when the powder magazine of the depot ship blew up, the depressing discovery was made that the stones at the bottom of the 'island' were slowly sliding down an incline on the sea-bed—a process, which, if it were allowed to continue, would keep the engineers working for years before the 'island' was complete. Scott himself donned a diving suit and went down to see what could be done. His answer was as daring as it was ingenious—it was to transform the 'island' into a stone caisson or, in Scott's own words:

To send divers down; to chain and drag out from the centre of the turtle's back[1] by means of heavy derricks all the rock that had been dumped in; to place these rocks thus rescued outside the circle of the proposed cone, piling them up as a breakwater, and after excavating down to the original sand of the bottom and uncovering the original Race Rock, to fill this water hole with concrete in the form of a great disc up to the level of low water, and upon this concrete disc to build the granite cone [as a foundation for the lighthouse].

It had been hard enough labour to pitch the heavy stones down onto the ocean's bed; the task of raising them again was immense.

The first thing necessary under this new plan was the erection of a system of four derricks, placed equidistant around the extreme edge of the turtle's shell; their tops connected by heavy wire rope and their outboard, or seaside guides, were to be made of heavy chain, strong enough to stand not only the weight of the stones themselves, but the extra strain of loosening the stones from the jagged stones around them.

The placing of these derricks required three weeks of constant work, during which they fell twice, endangering the lives of the men. Although twenty of them were at work over this turtle back, a space of 100 × 125 feet, and although the derrick masts with their chain guys came crashing down among them as they stood on the slippery rocks, strange to say, no one was hurt.

Scott himself supervised the underwater work, often spending hours at a stretch at the foot of the rock while the divers with chains and slings manhandled the boulders one by one until the circular stone wall was 8 inches above low-water level. Work could now proceed on the inside of the wall during the relatively short periods of low water, and, of course, after it had been pumped dry. Within and at the bottom of the caisson a circular iron band was set, 60 feet in diameter and 3 feet deep, this being filled with concrete. Upon it another band of a slightly smaller diameter was set and also filled with concrete. The process was repeated until a solid platform projected itself above low water, the plinth-like character of the concentric layers preventing the mass from spreading. On this solid platform of iron, concrete and stone a massive conical granite pier was built, 30 feet high by 57 feet in diameter at the base. The lighthouse built upon this pier is of granite and comprises a two-storey house for the keepers from the centre of which rises a tower crowned by a fourth-order light, 67 feet above high water.

There was a near disaster during the building of the tower. A wooden barrack had been built to house the workmen and one day, as they were resting within it, a sudden squall blew up. Captain Scott, realizing that it

[1] Race Rock.

was no ordinary squall, ordered the men to leave the house and to lash themselves to the boom of a derrick. The men were not at all keen to leave the warmth and apparent safety of their shelter to be exposed to the cold and wet of the Atlantic, but it was as well that Scott insisted, for hardly had they left the wooden house than the wind awoke with a sudden violence, plucked it from the rock and threw it into the sea. Race Rock light first flashed its warning beam on New Year's Day, 1879.

The desolate shores of Oregon on the western coast of the United States are as rugged and as wild as can be found anywhere in the world, and the coast that lines the estuary of the Columbia river is a singularly terrible one, rising at places to a height of 1,500 feet. Hard jagged rocks rear from the water or lurk beneath the surface and the whole dreadful area is frequently obscured by mists or the smoke from the huge forest fires which are commonplace during the summer months. There had long been a demand for a lighthouse at the entrance to the Columbia, and this demand was brought to a head in 1878 after a series of tragic shipwrecks.

It was first intended that the light would be erected on the mainland, and Major Gillespie of the Corps of Engineers was put in charge of a survey, but his report recommended that the light should be situated on a lonely crag known as Tillamook Rock. Although the weather had prevented Gillespie from landing on the rock he had made a close inspection of it from the deck of a lighthouse tender and reported to the Lighthouse Board:

I was enabled . . . to approach sufficiently near to become convinced that the rock is large enough, and the only suitable place for the light. To be efficient, the light should be exhibited as low as is safe to have it; the headland is entirely too high, even on the lowest bench, and if located ashore, a costly road must be built. Though I could not make a landing, I am of the opinion that it is practicable to use the rock for a light station, and am desirous of being allowed to make the attempt.

Tillamook Rock is an isolated mass of hard basalt rising to a height of 120 feet above the water. It stands a mile off Tillamook Head and twenty miles south of the mouth of the river. The water around it ranges from 94 to 240 feet deep, and when the sea is raging the rock presents a daunting sight. The waves hurl themselves at its base with such terrific force that on breaking they send tons of water over the very summit of the peak to sweep down on the opposite side. It was on the top of this almost unapproachable crag that it was decided to build.

The plan for building was to land an initial small force of men on the rock with provisions for a stay of six months. These men were to erect living-quarters for themselves and then to level and enlarge the area of the summit by blasting. On 18 September 1879 a master-mason who had been employed on the building of Wolf Rock lighthouse made a landing on Tillamook to examine the ground. As he stepped onto the rock he slipped on its wet surface and as he did so a wave, as if it had been waiting for the opportunity, instantly grasped him and pulled him into the sea. He was never seen again. This disaster had unfortunate results, for it put public opinion against the scheme, making labour difficult to obtain. However, through the energy and resources of the superintendent of works, A. Ballantyne, plus the offer of extra high wages, a force of nine skilled quarrymen was assembled and eventually landed on the rock. This first landing was found to be so dangerous that it was decided to provide an alternative and less hazardous method of disembarking men and materials. A 4½-inch rope was secured to the mast of the supply vessel with its other end made fast to ring bolts driven into the summit of the reef. A traveller block to run on the rope had an endless whip passing from it through two other blocks secured on the ship and the rock respectively. On the travelling block a stout hook was rigged to take supplies and materials and, for the men, there was an improvised 'breeches-buoy' made from a pair of ordinary trousers and a life-belt. As the supply vessel was in constant movement it was never possible to keep the line taut and, as it alternately sagged and tautened, the traveller received at least one ducking on his journey.

When men, tools, supplies and materials had been landed the progress of the work depended entirely on the weather. While the wooden living-house was being built the men lived in a tent held down by stout lashings made fast to ring bolts. The tent was a small affair, measuring 16 feet long, 6 feet wide and 4½ feet high, and in this confined space Ballantyne and his nine men had to sleep, eat and find shelter from the all-too-frequent storms.

As soon as the more substantial living-quarters were built a site was levelled for the main derrick which was then landed and set up; then from this landing base a path was excavated to the living-quarters, and continued as a bench hewn right around the rock at a height of 90 feet. The whole mass of rock above this bench was to be blasted off, piece by piece, and levelled as a site for the lighthouse. The outer surface of the rock was found to be quite soft and this was removed with small charges of black powder, but the nucleus was extremely tough and impervious to black powder. By opening this hard rock with cartridges and then using large amounts of powder it was gradually reduced. The blasting was carried out with extreme care—only small sections being removed at a time. Any attempt to hurry the work could have resulted in cracking the main body of the rock which was to support the building. The holes drilled to receive the powder had to be perfectly dry, and during the many periods when surf and spray were curtaining the crown of Tillamook it was not possible to handle the powder at all. During these periods, which sometimes lasted for days on end, little work could be done and the men spent their time in gloom and boredom.

Early in January 1880 the coast of Oregon was attacked by a tornado of terrific violence. The sea hammered all sides of Tillamook simultaneously and the men could find no better refuge than their flimsy wooden house. Here they sat throughout the night, unable even to converse over the thunder of the waves which at times hammered the roof of their hut. It seemed as if the rock itself would be dashed away by the fury of the storm. At two in the morning came the terrifying crash of a gigantic sea accompanied by the sound of timber snapping and rending. The storehouse had been smashed like matchwood. Near panic resulted among the men—for if the store-house could go, their barrack might follow. The men determined to get out while they could to seek refuge on the crown of the rock, but Ballantyne, knowing that the tornado could whisk the men away like straws if they ventured into the open, arrested the panic by the sheer force of his personality and forbade the men to leave the hut. For ten days they waited, soaked by the water that continually flowed through every crack and crevice of their home. On the eleventh the storm abated but it was another fortnight before the supply ships could come up with fresh provisions. It is a tribute to the calibre of those nineteenth-century workmen that hungry, exhausted and completely fed-up as they were, not one of them asked to return home with the tender.

For the rest of the winter the weather was comparatively mild and by 30 May the great mass of rock that formed Tillamook's crown had been removed and the material for erecting the lighthouse landed without mishap. The construction of the tower, dwelling and fog-signal house presented no difficulty and was completed in February 1881, the light having been installed and lit some three weeks previously. The lighthouse comprises a group of keepers' dwellings that surround a square light tower 48 feet high, the light itself shining 132 feet above high water. Tillamook lighthouse is one of the most exposed in the world and no year passes but it is assaulted by severe storms. Massive though the building is, it suffers constant damage from the buffetings of the sea. Some idea of the force of the Pacific at this point can be gained from the official report of a storm that struck the rock in 1886:

... the sea from the south-west broke over the rock, throwing large quantities of water above and on the building. The roofs on the south and west sides of the fog-signal room, and on the west side of the building, were crushed in. ... The concrete covering on the top of the rock around the building was broken, and a brick parapet filling in a low place outside the fence, at the south-east corner, were carried away. A mass of the filling weighing half-a-ton was thrown over the fence into the enclosure. Three 730-gallon water-tanks filled with water, at the west end of the building, were broken from their fastenings and piled against the fence.

The total cost of building this station was $123,492—less than the cost of only one of the fine ships the rock had claimed—while the number of lives it has saved must be immense.

Plate 9. The new Dungeness lighthouse, completed 1966.
(*Central Electricity Generating Board*)

Plate 10a. Grundkallen lighthouse (Sweden), an example of the Swedish technique of telescopic caissons for lighthouse construction.

Plate 10b. Launching the caisson unit for Grundkallen lighthouse.

14

The American Seaboard Illuminated

BALLANTYNE'S SUCCESS ON Tillamook Rock brought him fame and respect in the world of lighthouse builders and in the following year he was selected by the Lighthouse Board to tackle another wicked sea-swept rock on the American coast. The North-west Seal Rock is one of a number of hazards, some lurking beneath the sea, some towering above it, that are collectively known as St George's Reef and which lie opposite Crescent City, California. North-west Seal Rock is composed of a number of different types of stone which have but three qualities in common: they are extremely tough, very brittle when subjected to blasting, and as slippery as glass underfoot. The shape of the rock is an oval with a central ridge that falls gently to the north but steeply on its other sides; its sea-level area is 46,000 square feet and it rises to a maximum height of 54 feet. The sea often sweeps over the crest of North-west Seal and yet in order to clear a large enough area for a foundation it was necessary to excavate at a point 30 feet below the crest. There was nowhere on the rock where store-rooms or living-quarters could safely be sited and it was known that from a dead calm sea the top of the rock could be swept by powerful breakers within the space of three hours. This highly unfavourable spot was where Ballantyne was instructed to build and it is hardly surprising that his first job was to recruit as many as possible of those stalwarts who had toiled with him on Tillamook.

The nearest landing-place on the mainland was Crescent City, some thirteen miles away, but the approach to it is encumbered by so many submarine rocks and shoals that it could only be safely used for three months of the year. It was decided, therefore, to house both men and materials in a schooner moored near by, and for the purpose the *La Ninfa*, a topsail schooner of 127 tons, was chartered. A new ship, built for the strenuous job of carrying copper ore on the coast of South America, *La Ninfa* was altered and modified to make her suitable for the job in hand. In April 1883 she was towed out to the rock and secured to well-anchored spar buoys that had been prepared for her.

Following the success of his improvised 'breeches-buoy' on Tillamook, Ballantyne decided to use the same method for getting on and off North-west Seal, but this time a larger, stronger and more efficient rig was installed between ship and rock. *La Ninfa* was moored some 350 feet away and it was over this distance that men and materials had to travel. The traveller-block resembling a miniature bogey was made of boiler-plate, and instead of a hook for goods and a pair of trousers for men, an iron cage was suspended from it which could transport six men at a time between ship and land. The cage, being engine-hauled, could make the return trip with a full load in three minutes. The shore end of the cable was fixed at some 60 feet above sea-level while the lowest end of its curve missed the water by no more than 15 feet; consequently when the cage was released from the rock it ran down at a considerable speed so that even in a heavy swell when the waves touched the lower part of the cable it was possible to time the descents and get the men on board the schooner without wetting even their feet. Thus it was that when the work-ing party got used to this rather alarming method of retreat they would stay at work until the sea was up to the working level and then, after hastily lashing their tools to the ring-bolts provided, leave the rock in two or three parties and within minutes all would be safely aboard the *La Ninfa*.

Most of the rock levelling was carried out with high-explosive, large quantities of which were kept in a magazine built from heavy timber, secured on the very top of the rock with a network of 4-inch cables; even this was often shifted bodily as an occasional wave broke over the 50-foot summit of the rock. By August 1883 the foundations had been blasted roughly into shape and the rest of the season was taken up with hand finishing the surface.

In the following year the 70-foot-high circular base, consisting of over 11,000 cubic feet of granite, had been built and, after many delays caused by the reluctance of Congress to supply the necessary money, North-west Seal Rock was crowned with a magnificent lighthouse. It is a square granite tower with a projecting stair cylinder, the lantern being 146 feet above high water.

In Delaware Bay, some three and a half miles from the shore, is situated a huge shoal nearly 6,000 feet long and 1,300 feet wide, known to mariners as 'Fourteen Foot Bank' because of its dangerous shallowness. In 1876 the shoal had been marked by a lightship, but owing to the prevalence of floating ice in the area she could not stay on station during the winter—a time when a light was most needed. It was therefore decided by the United States Lighthouse Board to replace the lightship with a permanent tower which would be built on a concrete-filled cast-iron caisson. The previous year had seen the disaster of the first attempt to sink a caisson on Rothersand Shoal and long and serious consideration was given to how the task would be carried out on Fourteen Foot Bank. Many methods were considered by the Board, but in 1883 the plans put forward by the Board's chief engineer, Major D. P. Heap, were adopted. Heap proposed the construction and sinking of a cast-iron cylinder, 73 feet in height with a diameter of 35 feet, to be composed of $1\frac{1}{2}$-inch cast-iron plates, each 6 feet high with 6-inch horizontal and vertical flanges by which they would be bolted together. These flanges were to be accurately faced so that the joints would be water-tight. In December 1884 the government invited tenders for building the cylinder from materials supplied by them and sinking it 23 feet into the shoal; the bidders were not required to follow any particular plan in the process of sinking the caisson, but the successful contractor was bound to lodge a substantial deposit with the government to insure against its loss. Messrs Anderson and Barr, a New York firm of civil engineers, won the contract with a proposal to sink the cylinder through the pneumatic process.

First of all a square working caisson was built on which it was intended to place the cylinder. The caisson was of wood, 40 feet square, 5 feet thick with walls 7 feet high along the four sides. It was roofed at the top and open underneath, all the joints being waterproofed with caulking and mineral pitch. Running down from the centre of the 'roof' through the inside was a circular air-shaft, 5 feet in diameter. The completed structure resembled an upside-down box with a rim to form a cutting edge when resting on the sand.

On the 'roof' and around the central air-shaft the caisson proper was built up to an initial height of 18 feet and, after ballasting, the composite wood and iron structure was towed into position. Into the annular space between the cylinder walls and the air-shaft, concrete was laid to a depth of 9 inches and the sinking of the combined units was effected by letting water in through 6-inch valves. Box and cylinder descended slowly and evenly, but on touching the bottom heeled over to come to rest with a list of twelve degrees. The lower side of the cylinder's top edge was but inches from the surface of the sea—a nudge from the current, or even the wind, would have eliminated the small margin which kept out the water and the Rothersand disaster would have been repeated.

The engineers lost no time. While the tugs were sent post-haste to the shore to bring out cargoes of stone rip-rap, the engineers improvised large pockets on the elevated section of the cylinder's interior which were filled with the rip-rap as it arrived on the tugs. Gradually the structure righted itself and before the weather, scour or any other phenomenon could move it, the water was pumped out of the cylinder section and replaced with concrete, the weight of which induced the cutting edge of the wooden caisson to bury itself well into the sand. All danger of further canting was now gone but the upper edge of the cylinder, still perilously near the water, was liable to be submerged by a rough sea. No time was lost, therefore, in bolting two further sections of cylinder wall into place, thus bringing the rim some 20 feet above high water. An air-lock was fitted to the central air-shaft, and the working-chamber, having been pumped dry, was filled with compressed air. It was, of course, only necessary to increase the height of the air-shaft to keep pace with the rising level of concrete as the latter was built up within the cylinder. Inside the wooden 'box caisson', which, through the combined weight of cylinder, concrete, machinery and itself, was already well below the surface of the underwater sand, three gangs of eight men worked eight-hour shifts around the clock. They wore hats fitted with candle-holders in which burned ordinary paraffin-wax candles. The sand was conveyed from the working-chamber to the outside through a 4-inch pipe provided with two cocks, one in the chamber, and the other outside. Sinking progressed at the rate of one or two inches an hour, and after two weeks of continuous work the wooden cutting edge of the caisson had penetrated 18 feet into the sand, while the concrete had reached a depth of 37 feet within the cylinder. On 18 August, after just one month of digging and concreting, the required depth of 33 feet had been achieved. The cutting edge was then tightly under-rammed, the working-chamber packed tight with sand and the air-shaft filled with concrete. While the sinking operations were in progress, another gang of men were engaged in dumping 6,000 tons of rip-rap overboard and around the base of the cylinder to secure it from the movements of the current. The result was a circular rock rising from the ocean's bed as solid as any that Nature could provide.

Upon this was built the most picturesque lighthouse that can be found in mid-ocean—a charming three-storeyed, gabled dwelling house with a small tower attached (see Plate 5b). The erection of this lighthouse was a brilliant achievement—the work was done from start to finish in under two years, and of the allocated $175,000 the contractors were able to return $50,000 to the government—i.e., more than a quarter of the sum tendered.

The success of the operations on Fourteen Foot Bank persuaded the United States Lighthouse Board to use the same method to build a lighthouse on Diamond Shoals, a long sandbank extending some eight miles seaward from Cape Hatteras, North Carolina. So numerous are the shoals hereabouts that navigators gave the whole area as wide a berth as possible, and to help them to do so at night a stone light-tower was put on the Cape in 1798. It was replaced in 1870 by a brick tower with a granite base, 190 feet high, at the time the tallest lighthouse in the country. It soon became evident that the light on Cape Hatteras was insufficient and it was decided to place a lightship on near-by Diamond Shoals; this was done in 1824, but before long the lightship was washed away from its moorings and had to be towed back to its station and re-secured. This happened several times but finally, in 1827, the ship was driven ashore near Ocracoke Inlet and wrecked.

Nothing further was done about Diamond Shoals until, in 1851, in response to a report from the United States Navy that 'there is much required off the point of Hatteras shoal a fog bell that can be heard at some distance', Congress made appropriation for a 'floating bell beacon on Cape Hatteras, outer shoal'. In the following year a bell-boat was positioned on Diamond Shoals but within four months it had disappeared. Thirty years later a whistling buoy was moored there and in 1884 a gas buoy of which it was later reported that it 'remained in position but a few months and has since been drifting about the Atlantic. . . . It is evident that a buoy cannot be maintained at this point.'

In 1889 Congress authorized the construction of a lighthouse on Diamond Shoals and a caisson 54 feet in diameter by 45 feet high was built at Norfolk and towed to the site where it was grounded in 22 feet of water. The scour of the current caused it to sink out of level with one edge only a few feet from the water. Attempts to right it were frustrated by a rising sea and seven days later a storm carried away the machinery and broke the caisson in two. Work was abandoned. In 1894 the project was again examined and as an initial measure a skeleton iron frame on wrought-iron piles with large discs at their ends was floated out to the site on a pontoon and placed in position. From this, exploratory borings were made into the shoal to a depth of 105 feet as a guide to the nature of the foundations. What was found must have been discouraging, for a lightship was again placed on Diamond Shoals and it was not until 1966 that a lighthouse was at last erected.

In April 1906 an earthquake on the Pacific coast wrecked a number of United States lighthouses, among them the fine old tower on Point Arena. This was rebuilt in reinforced concrete—the first time that this material was used by the United States Lighthouse Board.

Today the United States spend $10,000,000 a year on their lighthouses, maintaining 527 manned stations as well as 26,800 other aids to navigation.

15

Progress in West and East

HE TURN OF the century saw many important developments in the
science of pharology, the most significant of which was described
by Dr J. A. Fleming, in a letter to *The* London *Times* on 3 April
1899:

During the last few days I have been privileged to make a close examination of
the apparatus and methods employed by Signor Marconi in his remarkable
experiments between South Foreland and Boulogne, and at the South Foreland
lighthouse was allowed by the inventor to make experiments and transmit
messages from the station there established, both to France and to the lightship
on the Goodwin Sands, which vessel has now been equipped for sending and
receiving ether wave signals. Throughout the period of my visit, messages, signals, congratulations and jokes were freely exchanged between the operators
sitting on either side of the English Channel and automatically printed down in
telegraphic code signals on a paper slip at the rate of twelve to eighteen words
a minute!

Marconi has thus placed a lightship on the Goodwins in instant communication, day and night, with the South Foreland lighthouse, and a touch of a key
on board the lightship suffices to ring a bell in a room at the South Foreland
lighthouse, *twelve miles away*, with the same ease and certainty with which one
can summon the servant to one's bedroom at an hotel! An attendant now sleeps
hard by the instrument at South Foreland and if at any moment he is awakened
by the electric bell rung from the lightship he is able to ring up in turn the
Ramsgate lifeboat and, if need be, direct it to the spot where its services are
required within a few minutes of the call for help. In the presence of this enormous practical and important feat alone, and of the certainty with which communication can now be established between ship and shore without costly cable
or wire, the scientific criticisms which have been launched by other inventors

against Signor Marconi's remarkable methods have failed altogether in their appreciation of the practical significance of the results he has now brought about. . . .

Because of the technical knowledge required of the light-keepers to operate and maintain wireless apparatus, it did not find favour at the time and the system of telegraph cables between some lighthouses and the shore was retained in spite of their tendency to break in bad weather. It was not until wireless telephony was developed that lighthouse authorities again turned to wireless and today nearly all rock lighthouses are equipped with a radio telephone. This innovation, plus the fitting of radio receivers in ships, led to an invention that was the forerunner of the modern radio-beacon—the so-called 'talking beacon' invented by the Stevenson family. A voice on an ordinary gramophone record gave out the name and situation of the lighthouse and then counted up to thirty. This record, continuously played and transmitted by the lighthouse, was picked up by the navigators of ships in the vicinity, who could then obtain a directional bearing on the signal.

Since Fresnel invented his lens lights there was no major improvement in lighthouse illumination for over eighty years until, in 1901, Arthur Kitson invented a new type of burner in which, instead of the oil being vaporized at the wick and burning as an open flame, it was converted into vapour under pressure in a container and mixed with air to form an inflammable gas which burned in an incandescent mantle. The container in which the oil was vaporized was a coiled copper tube placed above the mantle. The coil was initially heated by a blow-lamp until the system was working after which the mantle supplied enough heat to maintain the flow of oil vapour. Kitson's apparatus produced three times the light of the ordinary wick-burning lamp for the same amount of oil. The Kitson burner was developed by David Hood in 1921 to burn petro-leum vapour and is used today in situations where the use of electricity is impracticable.

In 1906 Nils Gustav Dalén produced his Dissolved Acetylene Gas Burner which is still the normal method of illuminating unwatched lights in the absence of electricity. The gas is pressurized into cylinders and burned either as an open flame or in an incandescent mantle automatically controlled by a time switch or a light-valve—the latter also being the invention of Dalén. A metal rod, coated with lamp-black to improve its light-absorbing properties, is connected at its lower end to a small lever that operates a valve controlling the supply of gas to the burner. Around this rod are three other copper rods with highly polished surfaces which, having no light-absorbing properties themselves, reflect what light they receive back onto the central rod. At daybreak the light warms the black rod which, expanding, operates the lever and closes the valve. The black rod is so arranged that it can only expand longitudinally. The operating of the valve is, of course, a gradual process and so the supply of gas, and consequently the intensity of the light, diminishes as daylight increases. As dusk falls the reverse process takes place. The valve is gradually opened to release gas to the burner which is fitted with a by-pass so that a dim light is shown that intensifies with the approach of night. The great advantage of the light-valve over the time switch is that it will operate automatically not only at dusk but at the onset of mist, fog or heavy clouds.

The principle of Dalén's valve is still employed although various refinements have been made to the original apparatus. The light-valve, as it is developed today, is so simple as to be almost foolproof. On the outside of the lenses are attached two glass containers, one painted black and the other left clear. Both are half-filled with ether or any similar readily-vaporizing liquid. They are connected together by a centrally pivoted metal shaft. The morning light heats the black container causing the ether to expand, thus forcing some of it into the other bulb. The extra weight in the clear bulb tilts the shaft, which closes a valve, cutting off the supply of fuel to the lamp. At sunset the reverse occurs.

In 1910 an automatic unwatched light was established in the Bristol Channel that incorporated a clockwork-controlled mechanism of singular ingenuity. Acetylene, which supplied the lantern, was stored under high pressure in a reservoir and emerged to feed the burners at 2 lb. per square inch. As it issued from the reservoir it was channelled into one of two cylinders, each of which was provided with an inlet and an outlet valve. The tops of the cylinders were closed with leather diaphragms which were arranged to actuate vertical rods, their upper ends connected to a pivoted rocker—rather like a beam engine. The gas entering one cylinder forced the leather diaphragm upwards, thus actuating the rod and pushing up one end of the rocker which in turn forced down the rod on the other end and exhausted the gas in the second cylinder. This reciprocal motion revolved the light and at the same time kept the clockwork, with which the light was started, fully wound.

In 1935 a lamp of 500,000,000 candle power was displayed at the Paris Exhibition and this remarkable light was later installed in Jument lighthouse. Its full power was only used during fog.

The early part of the twentieth century saw tremendous improvements in the lighting of Asian coastlines. Today the long coasts of China and Japan are as well-lighted as any in the world, but a look at a 'List of Lights' shows that by far the greater proportion of lighthouses in eastern waters was established since 1900. The Japanese went to the Stevensons for their first lighthouse; it was temporarily erected in England, fitted with optical apparatus, dismantled and sent east. The Japanese, as is their way, took this lighthouse as a pattern and built copies of it all round their coasts.

The Chinese were late in lighting their coasts. Prior to 1868 their navigational aids were few and far between and lights were virtually non-existent. The natives seldom, if ever, resorted to night navigation and by day they relied on the pagodas, artificial mounds and stone beacons that were set up as aids to sailors. In 1868 a Customs Marine Department was set up under the administration of Sir Robert Hart who was given the title of 'Grand Guardian of the Heir Apparent of China and Inspector General of Maritime Customs'. Sir Robert was a sincere and conscientious man with an imaginative view of his responsibilities to the Chinese people and their government, and he took every opportunity of helping them in every way he could.

Within a few months of his appointment he persuaded the Chinese government to entrust him with the additional task of establishing navigational lights on the most dangerous and busy points of the coast. Starting with buoys, lightships and masthead lights suspended from tripods, Sir Robert provided, within seven years, a chain of sea-lights which made secure the approaches to the more important harbours. On his appointment a 'List of Chinese Lights' was non-existent; by 1876 it listed sixty-four lights of which nine were of the first order. Owing to the poor quality of Chinese labour, towers were built from cast-iron sections prefabricated in England. One lighthouse built by Sir Robert and which must have saved hundreds of lives since its establishment was on the wreck-infested Breaker Point, some forty miles east of Hong Kong. Writing in 1875, the engineer to the marine department said: 'There is no point of the coast-line where a sea-light is more urgently required than on Breaker Point.' It took five years to build the tower and during that time two more disastrous wrecks occurred—the British barque *Sally*, and the German brig *Peri* were both lost with all hands. The tower sent out its warning ray on 8 December 1880. It was a first-order occulting light of 8,000 candle power. In 1909 a vaporizing petroleum apparatus was installed giving 25,500 candles and in 1928 another new apparatus produced a flash of 618,000 candles.

In 1932 the station, manned by two European keepers and four subordinate native staff, was visited by seventy Communist 'troops' accompanied by thirty camp followers. The keepers, in an attempt to keep matters on a friendly basis, made tea for their visitors but, in the middle of the party, the rebels seized and tied up the whole staff together with their families. On being told of the serious consequences to ships at sea if the light was not lit, they released the Chinese staff on the grounds that they were workers—not imperialists. After looting the station of nearly everything except the lantern, they left taking with them the European keepers and their families (which included four small children). A ransom was demanded and paid, but although the women and children were released the two keepers were never heard of again.

Chilang Point, mid-way between Breaker Point and Hong Kong, is another dangerous spot on the Chinese coast which, before the establishment of a lighthouse, offered a good living to Chinese wreckers. When the light put an end to this source of income the wreckers turned pirate and carried out this profession under the noses of the light-keepers. In 1930 the captain of the Japanese vessel *Kito Maru*, having had his ship taken by pirates, jumped overboard and swam to the lighthouse from where he was able to watch his ship looted and sunk. Chilang Point was for many years the finest light in the East and one of the finest in the world. When first lit it was a first-order light of 490,000 candle power and was increased to 930,000 candle power in 1929. In 1923 a Chinese assistant keeper, one Lin A Yang, was drowned while coming on duty at Chilang Point. As a consequence his Chinese colleagues refused to sleep in the tower through fear of his spirit, and the only European keeper had to keep all the night watches until a priest could be brought from the mainland to exorcise the ghost.

Many of the inshore lighthouses of China are built of reinforced concrete—a material which in the early part of this century was beginning to replace the use of masonry in marine architecture. A good example of a light station of that period can be seen at Pendeen in Cornwall, and it is typical of a modern inshore establishment. Built in 1900 it comprises, in addition to the tower, three separate houses for the keepers and their families, each containing a living-room, three bedrooms, kitchen, scullery and outhouse, and each having its own garden. There are three electricity generating plants; one for use, one for stand-by and another for emergency.

On the outbreak of the First World War most of the sea-lights were extinguished, only to be put on for the movements of the fleets and convoys. Inevitably a great many ships were lost as a result, one of the first being the Hospital Ship *Rohilla* which went down in November 1914 with great loss of life. In December of the same year Scarborough lighthouse was severely damaged when the town was bombarded by German warships.

On 28 October 1915 the 10,850-ton cruiser H.M.S. *Argyll* collided with the notorious Bell Rock and was completely wrecked—fortunately without loss of life. The *Argyll*, having just completed a refit, had not finished the process of adjusting her compasses and was not on course when she struck Bell Rock. The lighthouse had been instructed to light up for the benefit of the *Argyll* but owing to some confusion it did not do so until too late.

The English Channel was relit on 13 November 1918.

16

The Revolution in
Construction Methods

A LIGHTHOUSE WAS built off the coast of Sweden in 1930 that was eventually to revolutionize the design and construction of off-shore lighthouses all over the world. By building a concrete caisson in harbour, towing it to its site and sinking it, the Swedish engineers led the way to the 'telescopic' concrete towers that are familiar today. Many light-vessels in Swedish waters have to be withdrawn during the winter season because of ice, and it was for this reason that the Swedish Board of Navigation embarked on a plan in 1930 to replace ten of their lightships with permanent towers.

The first of these was built a little less than a mile from Trälleborg harbour on the southern coast of Sweden at a depth of 20 feet. A coffer-dam was built in Trälleborg within which was cast a caisson of reinforced concrete with a bottom diameter of 46 feet tapering upwards through 38 feet to a diameter of 9 feet, the inside being divided into eight watertight compartments. This was towed to the site, fitted with working scaffolds and sunk into place by filling it with water. Sand was then poured into it to 10 feet below sea-level, the remaining water pumped out to be replaced with concrete. A hollow space beneath the bottom of the caisson was then filled with grout pumped through iron pipes previously fitted. On this solid base was erected a reinforced concrete tower topped with a cast-iron lantern. As a protection against scouring and collision with ships, rip-rap was piled up to 10 feet below sea-level. The lighthouse is equipped with electric light with an acetylene lamp as a stand-by. Power is supplied through a submarine cable connected to the shore. The unmanned light is controlled by switches from the pilot's office on the mainland.

The Kalmar Strait off the south-eastern coast of Sweden is some eighty miles long and narrows to a width of about a mile and three-quarters. The many shoals and shallows, the strong currents and the drifting winter ice make it very difficult to navigate at night, especially at its narrowest part near Kalmar itself, which, for some three miles, dwindles to a width of about 90 yards and a depth of 25 feet.

During the years 1939–41 no less than five wave-swept lighthouses were erected near to this channel. All five sites were dredged to a level of 26 feet and levelled off with crushed stone. Meanwhile, five reinforced concrete caissons, each one divided into six watertight compartments, were built on shore. When complete, the caissons were towed to their various sites and lowered by filling two of their compartments with water. The six compartments of each caisson were then filled with concrete and stone; and, by means of previously fitted iron pipes, the crushed stone levels on which they stood were injected with concrete. On these foundations the light towers were erected.

It is sad to relate that while the Swedish engineers were further improving their shipping lanes by practically mass-producing lighthouses, the principal European combatants in the Second World War were doing their utmost to destroy those of their opponents. The wave-swept lighthouse, devoid of defence, was easy prey to the dive bomber in search of a little target practice. The plight of the keepers under such attacks is fearful to contemplate. With no refuge, avenue of retreat, means of retaliation or chance of relief, they could only hope that the slender form of the lighthouse would defeat the aim of the attacker. Many fine towers were destroyed with much loss of life, including St Catherine's lighthouse which in June 1943 suffered a direct hit which killed all three keepers. Lighthouses also came under attack from patrolling fighter pilots who made the lantern their target—the lenses of the famous Wolf Rock light were shattered by aerial cannon fire in March 1941 and Grace Darling's old home on Longstones was severely damaged by a bomb in the same year. The Casquets, which passed into German hands in 1940, became a regular target for British fighters who destroyed the light on several occasions. Although heavily fortified by the Germans the Casquets were also visited by British Commando units on more than one occasion whose purpose was the destruction of its important radio-beacon. Radio telephone transmitters were installed in most isolated light-stations during the war and were afterwards retained.

The rebuilding of Europe's shattered cities after the end of the Second World War was carried out in the face of a great scarcity of building materials and labour. As a consequence many new techniques and constructional methods were used which have since become standard practice.

The designers of lighthouses, for the obvious reason that their edifices are usually subject to far greater stresses and strains than are other buildings, tended, for centuries, to be wary of materials and techniques that had not been proven by the test of time. When the French Commission des Phares embarked on a programme to replace the many lighthouses on their coasts which had suffered through bombardment or dilapidation it was decided that pre-stressed concrete, which had never before been used in lighthouse construction, would give the towers greater strength, reduce cracking and effect considerable economies in labour and materials. A concrete construction is 'pre-stressed' when permanent stresses have been applied to it before the varying loads that it will be called upon to withstand have been exerted. This is done in such a manner that the stresses resulting from the permanent stresses and from the stresses due to load may be withstood indefinitely by the material used in the construction.

It was realized by the French engineers that the first application of this method would be in the nature of an experiment, so Berck lighthouse near Boulogne was chosen because, being a tall tower in a very exposed position, it was ideal as a test for the new process.

The tower is a cylinder consisting of three parts—the foundation, the base and the tower. The foundation is a circular layer of concrete surrounded by a wall of metal sheet piles, while the base is a 20-foot-diameter concrete cylinder, 18 inches thick and 18½ feet high, pre-stressed with vertical steel bars. Thirty-six vertical cables of varying lengths are anchored into it. The tower itself, which is 106 feet high, is built entirely of pre-cast units pre-stressed together, the main elements being concrete hoops, 18½ feet in outside diameter, 8 inches thick and 4 inches high; in each of them a ring-band was embedded consisting of thirty-two 1-inch diameter rods stressed to 54 tons to the square inch. The hoops are at vertical intervals of 3 feet 9 inches, the spaces between them consisting of three courses of pre-cast units. After being put into position with a crane the hoops and stones were pre-stressed vertically by the cables anchored in the base which pass through grooves in the units and holes in the hoops. Nine of the cables reach 104 feet up to the top of the tower, nine reach a height of 78 feet, nine 52 feet and nine 26 feet. All the cables were drawn tight by means of hydraulic jacks to a stress of 20 tons each. The completed lighthouse was thus a cylinder, 105 feet high, 18 feet in diameter horizontally stressed by the pre-stressed hoops and vertically stressed by thirty-six, then twenty-seven, then eighteen, then nine cables exerting between them a total strain of 720 tons. The result is immensely strong and as capable of resisting the horizontal pressures of wind as the mightiest of granite towers.

Lying a mile east of Nidingen Island, six miles off the coast of Sweden, there is a peculiar reef. Although there are no tides in Swedish waters the reef, which is generally submerged, has the habit of raising itself some 6 feet above sea-level. This is because certain combinations of strong gales and currents tend to pick up the loose boulders that surround the bottom of the reef and throw them up on the rock. Combinations of other winds and races throw them back in the sea and the reef is again submerged. In 1945 a lighthouse was built here on a reinforced concrete caisson foundation which was fabricated at Gothenburg, thirty miles from the site. The site was dredged level and a circular hole, 17 feet deep, dug down to the firm bottom to receive the caisson which was lined with iron at its base and fitted with a timber bottom. When the caisson was sunk, divers removed the bottom and adjusted its level by digging; it was then filled with concrete and used as the foundation of the lighthouse proper.

Using their, by now, well-tried method of the floating caisson, Swedish engineers, in 1947, built another lighthouse in the open sea twelve miles off the southern point of the Baltic island of Öland. In this instance the caisson, before being towed to its site, was fitted with living-rooms for the engineers and workmen, a heating system, sanitary arrangements, the electric plant, construction machinery, a temporary light, fog bell and radio telephone.

These important developments in Sweden were soon to be rivalled on the other side of the Atlantic when in 1957 the United States Coastguard embarked on a long-term plan to replace their lightships with permanent structures. The United States Lighthouse Board in a report made in 1890 said: 'The purpose of a lightship is to do the work of a lighthouse where one is necessary, but where it has not been erected because of the great difficulty, not to say expense, of such a structure.' Indeed, it can safely be said that a lighthouse is a far better means of displaying a navigational light than is a light-vessel, except in situations where sands tend to shift or where the site is difficult to build upon. The main advantages of the lighthouse over the lightship can be summarized as follows: fewer crew are required; maintenance is easier; more accurate positioning is possible; unattended operation can be resorted to; conditions are better for the light-keepers; and last, but by far not least, the lighthouse is a stable structure, ideal for modern electronic devices which require directional aerials. The light itself can be permanently directed towards the horizon without the use of the complicated self-levelling mechanisms which are needed on a lightship.

Until the late 1950s, lighthouse building in the United States was mainly confined to shore stations or to comparatively shallow waters, but in 1957 a feasibility study was made which considered the various factors, economic and technical, connected with the replacement of the twenty-five lightships by fixed lights. The great advances in building techniques in general and in marine construction in particular led the United States Coastguard to implement the plan to replace their lightships, and after considering various constructional methods they decided on template structures as being the most economic means for the purpose. This consists of a platform supported by a framework of four steel pipe members, horizontally, vertically and diagonally braced with smaller pipe members. The four-legged framework, called the jacket, rests on the ocean-bed and the main pipe members act as templates through which hollow steel legs are driven until they reach bedrock. These inner legs are then filled with concrete while the annular space between them and the jacket pipes is grouted.

The first two such structures were built·in 1961 to replace the light-vessels in Buzzards Bay, Massachusetts, and Brenton Reef, Rhode Island; later the same method was used to light the hitherto unconquered Diamond Shoals.

The jacket of the Buzzards Bay light is 82½ feet high, 50 feet square at the top, 60 feet square at the bottom, and projects 13½ feet above low-water level; the overall height from the top of the tower to the bedrock ends of the piles is 438 feet. The light of 10,000,000 candle power is visible at sixteen miles distance. There is a helicopter landing area on the topmost deck.

A number of these structures have been erected off the coasts of the United States and a description of the Chesapeake light-station is a good example of this method of construction.

This lighthouse, built in 1965, stands fourteen miles off Cape Henry, Virginia. All the units of the tower, including the deckhouse, were prefabricated on shore, loaded onto barges and towed to the site. Here they were taken in hand by a huge marine pile-driving rig consisting of a barge, 70 feet by 150 feet by 13 feet deep, which could be jacked up over the waves on legs 6 feet in diameter and which carried a crane of 100-ton capacity.

The 70-foot-square jacket section is 64 feet high with 39-inch pipe legs at each corner, while the bracing members are 18 inches in diameter. All members near the water line are wrapped with wrought-iron corrosion shields. To sink the jacket legs into the sand, water jets were fitted inside them, which, operating under pressure, cut away the soil to allow the jacket to settle 12 feet into the sea-bed. The water jets then being removed, 33-inch-diameter open-ended pipe piles were dropped into the jacket pipes and driven to a tip elevation of 228 feet below low-water level. One splice was required on each pile. Sand and water were removed from the piles to a depth of 60 feet below water level and the resulting space filled with concrete. The annular spaces between the 39-inch jackets and the 33-inch piles were then pressure-grouted with the result that jackets and piles were rigidly locked together.

The landing deck and maintenance deck were then welded to the piles, the oil and water tanks welded together as a single unit, also being welded

Plate 11a. The cabin unit for the Royal Sovereign lighthouse under construction in Newhaven harbour. (*Christiani and Nielson*)

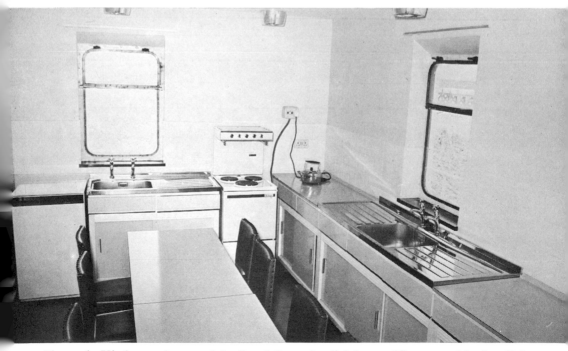

Plate 11b. Kitchen and mess of the Royal Sovereign lighthouse. (Compare with plate 6b.) The tower also contains a television room and a hobbies room. (*Christiani and Nielson*)

Plate 12. Wolf Rock lighthouse in a heavy sea. It is not unusual for the waves completely to envelop the tower. (*M.O.D. (Air) Crown Copyright 1971*)

to the main structure. Each weld was radiographed before the next one was made. The deckhouse, already installed with fittings, fixtures, plumbing and electric wiring, was delivered in four separate sections, lifted by the crane and put into position. The lantern tower with its 50-foot radio antenna was delivered in one piece. From start to finish the fabrication and erection of Chesapeake lighthouse took nine months at a total cost of $1,509,750.

The new lighthouse at Dungeness in Kent, one of the most modern in the world, was built by an entirely novel method (see Plate 9). Rising 130 feet from its base, the tower is constructed from twenty-one pre-cast concrete rings which interlock with each other, top and bottom. The rings are vertically stressed together with cables running through holes from top to bottom of the tower where they are anchored under tension. The base of the shaft is a spiral ramp while the two top rings contain sixty honeycomb-like holes which house foghorn emitters. The light is unattended.

17

The Telescopic Principle

ASSUMING THE FEASIBILITY of towing a large structure out to sea and placing it on its site, the advantages of pre-fabricating a wave-swept lighthouse in the shelter of a harbour are obvious. By this method, all the difficulties that faced the early lighthouse builders are eliminated—the danger to the workmen, the long delays due to bad weather, the restriction of the work to the summer season and the difficulty of communication between the site and the workshops ashore.

As we have seen, it was the Swedes who evolved the technique of making concrete caissons in harbour before towing them out to their sea positions; from this they developed the telescopic principle of lighthouse building—the most substantial technical advance in the science of building stone wave-swept towers since Rudyerd built on Eddystone. The method was first used in 1961 for the Grundkallen lighthouse off the coast of Sweden (see Plate 10a). Two closed-bottom caissons were built, one within the other, of a sufficient volume to allow them to float (see Plate 10b). Towed to the site, the combined unit was sunk onto the rock sea-bed, which had previously been levelled by blasting and covered with a layer of macadam. Water was then pumped below the inner caisson, causing it to float up, and the two units were locked together with concrete casting. The outer, foundation, caisson was then filled with gravel which was injected with mortar. During the same year the same method was used to build an unmanned tower off the Swedish coast, forty miles from Stockholm. In this case three telescopic units were used and the completed set was towed out and bedded within four months of the commencement of the work. To have built a masonry tower in mid-ocean would have taken the old lighthouse builders as many years.

The construction of the Kish Bank lighthouse in Dublin Bay represented a spectacular development in the use of telescopic caissons. Twice the size of any tower hitherto built by this method, it ranks as one of the most daring feats of modern engineering. Kish Bank, which is only two fathoms below low water at its shallowest point, is one of a continuous series of shoals which extend from the entrance of Dublin Bay to Wexford—a distance of some eighty miles. Ships bound for Dublin or Dun Laoghaire must sail around the banks to enter the bay, and from 1811 until recently the shoal was marked by a lightship. In 1840 Alexander Mitchell was called in to erect a screw-pile lighthouse to replace the lightship, but his screw piles were, to use his own word, 'prostrated' in a gale in 1842.

In 1962 the Commissioners of Irish Lights decided that it was feasible to put a permanent light on Kish Bank and instructed their engineers to call for tenders for its design and construction. At first it was considered that an open-work pile structure would be suitable, but this idea was abandoned in favour of the entirely different plan put forward by the Swedish firm of Christiani and Nielson. Their proposal for a large telescopic caisson offered many advantages including a lantern 100 feet above sea-level, minimum maintenance cost, long life, spacious accommodation for the keepers, safety during construction and extensive prefabrication. In the meantime, drilling tests on the bank were carried out to reveal that 300 feet of sand and silt had to be penetrated before solid rock was encountered. This was an important consideration in deciding between the two proposed methods of building. To determine the density of the sand on the site a 'neutron depth moisture probe' was lowered into it through a thin tube of stainless steel. This, by measuring the spaces between the grains of sand, informed the engineers that the soil was firm enough to support the weight of a tower.

On the completion and acceptance of Christiani and Nielson's design a 1/60 scale model of the lighthouse was subjected to the weather conditions that could be anticipated on Kish Bank over a period of one hundred years; these would include, it was estimated, a worst wave forty-five feet high and a wind velocity of 125 miles per hour for a duration of two seconds at a time.

The lighthouse consists of two separate cylindrical units which, in construction and siting, were telescoped one inside the other. The outer cylinder, a caisson supporting the tower proper, consists of three concentric cylinders built onto a 3-foot-thick concrete base and interlocked by twelve radial walls; the central cylinder contains the light tower which is 112 feet high. The outer caisson section is 72 feet high, 104 feet in diameter and the combined units weigh 6,700 tons.

Construction started in a corner of Dun Laoghaire harbour in August 1963, the outer cylinder being completed by the end of the year. It was then floated and construction of the inner tower was begun. It seems that the lighthouse builder can never escape the attentions of his old enemy even when working in the apparent shelter of a harbour for, in December 1963, a storm of unforeseen intensity so disturbed the harbour water that the caisson was sunk and damaged beyond repair through grounding on an uneven surface. There being nothing for it but to start again, it was decided to roof the old caisson over for use as a pontoon on which the new one could be built. A one-inch layer of sand was spread over the roof of the old unit to prevent adherence and the base slab and walls of the new one built on it. When the weight of the two caissons was still such that it would float in the 18-foot depth of water in the harbour, the combined structure was towed into deeper water where the building of the inner cylinder was started and continued to the point where its weight would not prevent it floating off the pontoon; then, by pumping out the ballast water from the new structure, it was separated from the old in November 1964.

While the constructional work was in progress, divers, working in ten fathoms of water, built a 120-foot-diameter radial screed on the ocean's bed which they later used to form a 6-inch-thick level bed of gravel for the caisson to rest upon. In June the lighthouse was complete and on the 29th of that month it was towed to its site by two tugs and made fast to four previously prepared moorings, prior to being exactly positioned above its site. At this stage a strong wind sprang up, accompanied by a thick fog. One of the mooring lines broke so it was decided to sink the unit then and there, which was several hundred feet south of the intended site. Here it remained until 15 July when it was refloated and placed in its correct position. The lower part of the annular space between the outer wall of the caisson and the tower proper was then filled with sand by a dredger and the tower was raised by flooding the inner cylinder of the caisson with water. Sand and stones were filled into the space left by the tower while the remaining space between tower and caisson was filled with concrete. The Kish Bank lighthouse was equipped and handed over to the Commissioners of Irish Lights in November 1965. Crowning the tower, eleven floors above the sea, is a helicopter landing platform. The light is of the catoptric type giving 2,000,000 candle power which can be increased in fog to 3,000,000 candle power. Situated 94 feet above sea level, it can be seen for nearly twenty miles. The lighthouse is also equipped with 'Racon', a device that allows ships to distinguish and identify it on their radar screens.

Compared with the living-quarters of the old wave-swept towers, the keepers' accommodation on Kish Bank is luxurious. The four keepers have separate bedrooms, a lounge equipped with television, a hobbies room, a laundry, bathroom, and a kitchen with an electric cooker, refrigerator and a deep-freeze. There is central heating and air conditioning.

Although the telescopic caisson method of building lighthouses had been used before, the construction of the Kish Bank tower was a conspicuous and significant event in marine engineering. The building, transporting and placing of this huge and complex piece was carried out without a single engineering hitch—the only setbacks having been caused by exceptional and unforecast weather.

The unattended in-shore lighthouse at Tater-Dhu near Penzance in Cornwall is completely automatic as well as being fitted with remote-control equipment. The main light is a filament lamp giving 300,000 candle power through a revolving optic, and there is a secondary 7,000 candle-power red light which shines over the near-by Runnelstone Rocks. Both these lights are lit and extinguished by means of time switches fitted with a solar device which alters their timing to suit the varying times of sunset and sunrise. The lamp is supplied from the mains and in the event of a power failure, batteries, which can run the lamp for five days, are automatically brought into use. In the event of a longer failure the batteries can be recharged by a diesel-driven generator. There is a lamp-changing turret with five extra lamps that operates automatically if a lamp should fail. The tower, which is 45 feet tall, stands on a cliff some 70 feet above sea-level. It came into operation in 1965.

There is one drawback to the telescopic caisson system of building. The outer caisson has to support the entire weight of the lighthouse while it is being towed to its site and therefore it has to be very large indeed—far larger than is necessary when once the tower is bedded down. Again it was the Swedish engineers who provided a solution to this problem in the design of the Trubaduren lighthouse in 1968. The tower was built to its full height on shore with its caisson of the minimum height required to give it stability in its final position at sea. A temporary wall was then built around the top of the caisson of sufficient height to provide the required floating capacity. The whole unit was towed to its site and bedded, the temporary wall being removed by unbolting it from the caisson and opening two gate sections to allow the wall to be towed away for subsequent re-use. The caisson proper was then ballasted in the usual way. The advantages in this method of construction are threefold. First, there is a considerable saving in building costs; second, the smaller caisson offers less resistance to the wind, waves and ice; third, by building the tower to its full height ashore, the complicated operation of telescopic lifting is avoided. The operation of removing the wall from Trubaduren lighthouse took only four hours.

The year 1971 saw the completion of what is, up to now, the ultimate in lighthouse building. Early in 1966 the Corporation of Trinity House decided to erect a lighthouse in place of the *Royal Sovereign* lightship, which lies eight miles off Beachy Head in the English Channel. Tests made

Figures 1–9. Floating and siting the Royal Sovereign lighthouse
(courtesy of Messrs Christiani and Nielson)

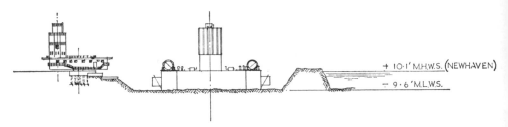

+ 10·1′ M.H.W.S. (NEWHAVEN)

− 9·6′ M.L.W.S.

Fig. 1 The telescopic caisson unit in the temporary dry berth in which it was built, with (left) the cabin unit on shore

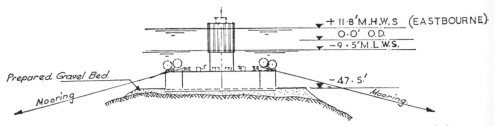

Fig. 2 The caisson unit, with upper tower telescoped, is floated for towing to site

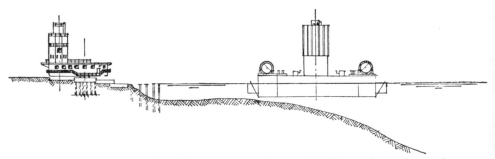

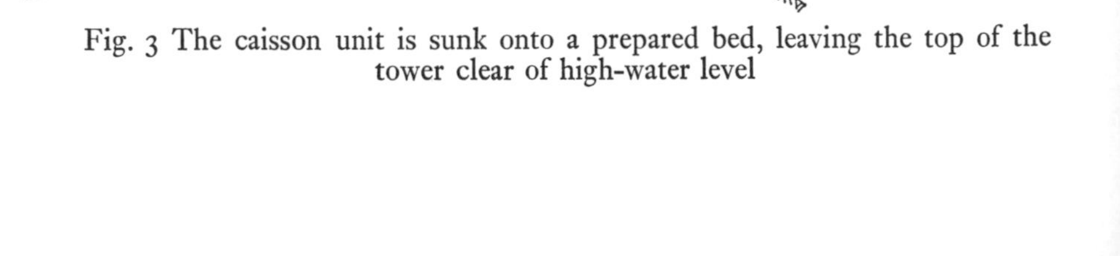

+ 11·8′ M.H.W.S (EASTBOURNE)

0·0′ O.D.

−9·5′ M.L.W.S.

Prepared Gravel Bed.

Mooring

− 47·5′

Mooring.

Fig. 3 The caisson unit is sunk onto a prepared bed, leaving the top of the tower clear of high-water level

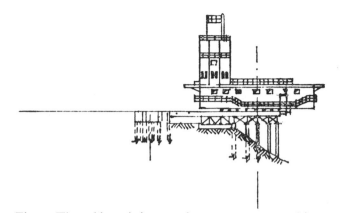

Fig. 4. The cabin unit is moved out onto a prepared jetty

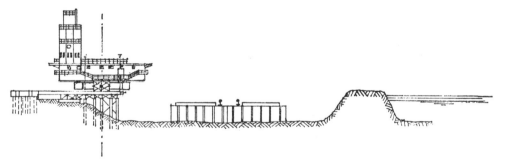
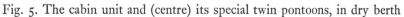

Fig. 5. The cabin unit and (centre) its special twin pontoons, in dry berth

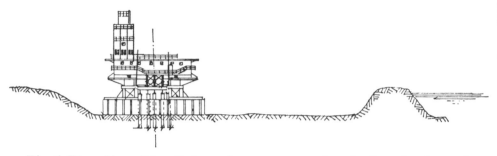

Fig. 6. The cabin unit is rolled onto its pontoons, ready to be floated and towed
to site

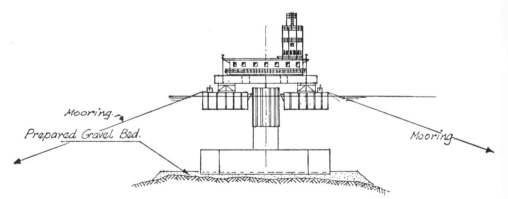

Fig. 7. The cabin unit in position, straddling the tower, with the pontoons partially
flooded to allow the cabin unit to fall with the tide directly onto the tower

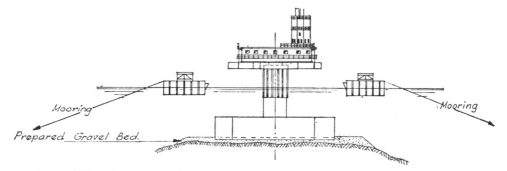

Fig. 8. The cabin unit positioned on the tower; the pontoons are now towed away

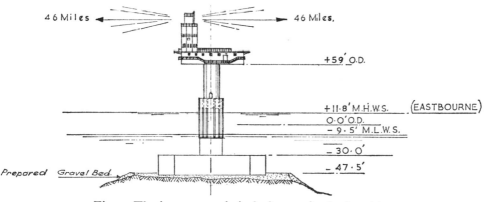

Fig. 9. The inner tower is jacked up to its final position

by the National Institute of Oceanography predicted that within periods of one hundred years and five hundred years, at least one wave could be expected of 46 feet and 53 feet respectively. As in the case of the Kish Bank lighthouse, it was at first intended to build an open-work steel tower of the template type, but a number of factors, in particular the unsuitability of the sea-bed for erecting piles and the 64-foot depth of water at high tide, persuaded the engineers to consider alternative designs. Again it was the firm of Christiani and Nielson that provided the answer with a plan for a concrete telescopic structure which they proposed to build in a temporary berth especially excavated in the beach near Newhaven harbour. The structure consists of a 73-foot-high concrete caisson on a hollow cellular concrete base, 162 feet in diameter, within which is telescoped a 70-foot tubular concrete tower supporting a concrete cabin and a steel light tower. The operation of siting the lighthouse was as follows:

1 The caisson and lower tower, with the upper tower telescoped within, it was floated to the site.
2 The caisson was sunk onto a prepared bed, leaving the top of the tower 4 to 5 feet clear of high water level.
3 The cabin (see Plate 11a), built as a separate unit, was then floated out on two rectangular pontoons and put into position straddling the tower. These pontoons were then partially flooded to allow the cabin to fall with the tide on to the tower.
4 The inner tower was jacked up some 50 feet taking the cabin up to its final position.
5 The wall of the outer tower was built up to its final level.

Construction began in April 1967, and by the spring of 1969 the caisson was ready to be sited. There was a serious hold-up in November 1967 when a force-nine gale broke through the temporary sea-wall specially built to protect the works, causing such chaos that it took three months to clear up the mess. Fortunately no damage was done to the half-built caisson. In August 1969 the caisson set was towed a quarter of a mile into the bay and temporarily bedded down in a position where it could be readily towed to its site. The reasons for this were twofold: firstly, to leave the construction site clear for the completion and floating of the cabin unit; secondly, because two sets of weather conditions were required to transfer the caisson from the construction site to its final site. A high spring tide was needed to move it from its berth while the towing and sinking operation required neap tides and at least two days without swell. The cabin was built on a pair of massive beams supported on piles with roller tracks set on them to allow the cabin to be rolled onto the pontoons.

While the work was proceeding, divers were preparing the sea-bed at the site, removing stones and boulders, levelling the sand, and laying a bed of gravel. This was done with a 70-foot screed-rail pivoted to a central concrete block running on a circular rail laid on twenty smaller concrete blocks, towed round by a launch on the surface. The screed rail was used both as a level check and to smooth out the gravel. The divers engaged on this difficult and exacting work were, like the old lighthouse builders, very much subject to the weather, being able to work on average only eight days in a month. The caisson was towed to the site area on 13 June 1970 and moored between eight marker buoys; by hauling on the moorings it was then positioned directly above the site. At this point a heavy fog gave the engineers a galling twelve-hour wait before work could be continued—a squall or heavy sea at that time could have spelt disaster to the whole operation for it was known that if the decks became awash the structure would lose stability and would probably founder. But all went well, the caisson being safely flooded and bedded down at 12 noon on the following day. The underside of the caisson consists of twenty cells, the walls of which formed edges that cut into the sand through its own weight. To prevent these edges from penetrating further than the required 6 inches a large bag of sand was positioned within the four corner cells; by washing sand out of each bag as required, the level of the structure could be controlled.

On 11 February 1971 the cabin was rolled onto the pontoons and taken to Portsmouth harbour where it waited until 15 May. It was then towed to the site and moored above the tower. Next, by a well-nigh incredible feet of manipulation, the 1,780-ton unit was positioned to within 5 inches of its correct position. The control that had to be exercised over this massive structure can only be described as four-dimensional; fore and aft movement, sideways movement, twist movement and vertical movement during the operation of threading the tower through the ring running through the cabin's centre; in addition there was, of course, the movement of the sea to take into consideration.

When the cabin unit was positioned, the pontoons were partially flooded allowing it to encircle the tower like a ring on a finger. Two tapered pins, 16 inches in diameter, were lowered from within the core of the cabin into holes previously placed in the tower, then as the tide fell the pins brought the two units together within a limit of $\frac{1}{4}$ inch. The high-tensile reinforcing bars of the inner cylinder were extended up through the core of the cabin section, stressed and grouted. Then the inner tower was jacked up by twelve 150-ton jacks and anchored to the top of the main, outer caisson. The space between the two towers was grouted and the outer tower built up to a further 12 feet to bring the landing platform to the required height. All that remained was to fit the building with equipment and services.

The lantern of the *Royal Sovereign* lighthouse comprises a catadioptric

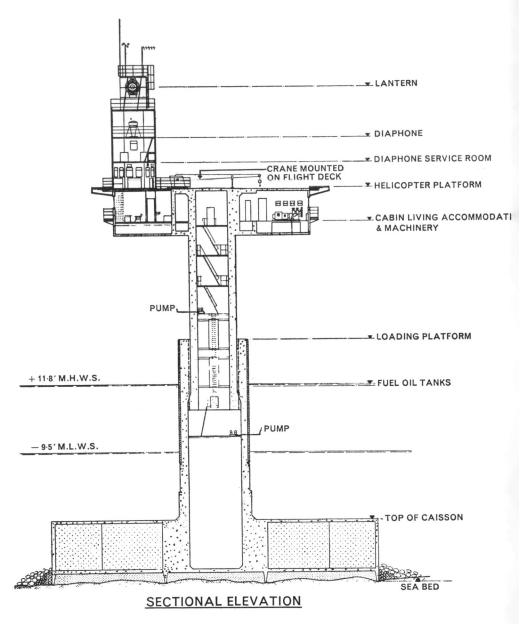

LANTERN

DIAPHONE

DIAPHONE SERVICE ROOM

CRANE MOUNTED
ON FLIGHT DECK

HELICOPTER PLATFORM

CABIN LIVING ACCOMMODATI
& MACHINERY

PUMP

LOADING PLATFORM

+ 11·8′ M.H.W.S.

FUEL OIL TANKS

PUMP

− 9·5′ M.L.W.S.

TOP OF CAISSON

SEA BED

SECTIONAL ELEVATION

Figure 10. Royal Sovereign lighthouse
(courtesy of Messrs Christiani and Nielsen)

lens rotating at one revolution a minute, producing a 2,500,000 candle-power flash of 0·52 seconds duration every twenty seconds with a range of twenty-eight miles. The light source is a 1,000-watt electric lamp which has an automatic four-position lamp changer with two reserve main lamps and a fourth, 500-watt, lamp for use with the emergency batteries. Beneath the lantern is an omni-directional Diaphone fog signal operated by compressed air provided by two diesel compressors. The crew consists of three keepers with a fourth man on leave. Like that in Kish Bank lighthouse, the accommodation can only be described as palatial when compared with the living space of the old towers (see Plate 11b).

18

The Light-keeper's World

INNUMERABLE TALES OF romance, of blood and of thunder in particular have been written about the men—and women—whose task it has been to keep the lights in sea-swept towers. These stories were especially popular in Victorian times and from them it would appear that, far from being a life of boredom and isolation, the light-keeper's lot seldom contained a dull moment. Murder, mayhem, suicide and sudden insanity would appear to have been commonplace on isolated rock stations—more than one keeper having been rumoured, for one reason or another, as having turned white-haired overnight. Many a little child, its parents having been murdered or kidnapped by wreckers, was, we are asked to believe, left alone to tend the light and (to judge by the illustrations) compelled to stand on the family Bible in order to reach the lantern. But sensational and fantastic as these stories may be, they contain a basis of truth, for any job that entails constant exposure to the forces of nature must have its dramas and its dangers, and when the job also involves long periods of isolation the dangers and dramas will be multiplied.

As recently as 1926 the keeper of Bembridge lighthouse went ashore for stores, leaving his fifteen-year-old daughter Ethel alone in the lighthouse. A violent storm blew up and he was unable to return for several days. Ethel, true to the tradition of the lighthouse keeper's daughter, lit and tended the lantern until her father was able to return. She became famous overnight as a minor Grace Darling and through the agency of *The Times* a collection was made on her behalf which reached the sum of £50. With the money a gold wrist watch was bought and suitably inscribed, the balance being put into shares until she was twenty-one.

Cases of keepers becoming homicidally insane are, fortunately, extremely rare, for the prospect of finding oneself suddenly confined on an isolated rock with a maniac would be enough to deter all but the least imaginative men from making the lighthouse service their career. The situation, however, is not unknown, for in Ockseu (China) lighthouse in December 1922, the principal keeper, a European, suddenly went insane and terrorized the whole establishment for several days before shooting dead his European assistant and himself. The two subordinate Chinese keepers kept the light going for twelve days before relief came. It is not recorded that their hair turned white overnight but, being ignorant and superstitious men, they were found to be in a state of gibbering terror and it is much to the credit of their sense of duty that they maintained the light.

In 1836 the lighthouse on Cape Florida was involved in an incident that contained all the ingredients for a full-length Western film. The second Seminole Indian war was in full swing when, early one morning, the keepers of Cape Florida, comprising a head keeper, assistant and a Negro servant, found the lighthouse under siege from a strong band of Indians. They retreated to the first floor from where they fought the attackers with rifle fire throughout the morning, killing and wounding many of them. After sustaining considerable losses the Indians concentrated their efforts in piling wood around the base of the tower and in the first-floor room. This they set alight and the flames, catching hold of the wooden floors one by one, drove the keepers further and further up the tower until they gained the lamp-room gallery. Here the Negro was shot dead and the assistant wounded before, in the nick of time and in the good old Western tradition, a government cutter arrived to save the day.

A tragi-comic incident occurred in 1928 on an isolated cay in the Bahamas which was then guarded by a beacon known as Double-headed Shot light. The keeper, who lived on the cay with his family, died suddenly. No relief was expected for several days and, because of the warm climate, the family were faced with the task of burying the body without delay. No grave could be dug as the islet is composed of hard rock, and the only suitable spot for interment was a natural hole in the rock. Into this the body was lowered in a standing-up position, a stone being placed over the top. During the makeshift ceremony a violent storm blew up and as the family made their way from the improvised tomb to the lighthouse they heard a loud report which made them turn their heads towards the grave, just in time to see the corpse shoot, head first, into the air like a rocket. The cavity chosen as the keeper's tomb was a blow hole! When the Imperial Lighthouse Service learned of this distressing episode they reacted in a typically bureaucratic manner. To meet such emergencies in the future they had four concrete graves built on the cay—two full-sized, two child-sized—with heavy concrete lids. Double-headed Shot light was closed before the graves were used.

There is a pathetic story of the keeper of Key West light, who after thirty-five years of service became so absorbed in his duty that he would not leave his task, even for a short vacation, labouring under the delusion that no one but himself could properly care for the light. On a certain very stormy night a ship was wrecked near the fort at Key West. The keeper, then nearly seventy years of age, excited by the prolonged whistle blasts of the unfortunate vessel, insisted that the wreck was due to the front range light being out, although it had just been examined by his son and found to be burning properly. In spite of his feeble condition the keeper procured a lantern and, resisting efforts to detain him, went on foot in the storm to the range light and satisfied himself that it was really burning.

Cases of light failure caused through neglect and error are rare enough to demonstrate that the world's lighthouse services have always attracted men of strong character and high calibre, and the low wages paid to them in the past seems to indicate that men chose a light-keeper's career because they preferred it to any other. Often the job of light-keeper has been a family affair with generations of sons following their fathers. A Henry Knott was appointed keeper to the South Forelands light in 1730 and his descendants gave 180 years' continuous service to sea-lights, the last of the line retiring in 1910. A Major George Elliot visited the South Forelands lighthouse in 1874 and found the keepers to be

. . . very intelligent men who seemed thoroughly to understand the magneto-electric machines, and who gave me an accurate account of their operation. One of them was by trade a watchmaker, and the other a stone-mason. The latter told me with evident pride that he had laid all the stone at the Bishop's Rock near the Scilly Islands, one of the most exposed stations in the English Service, and had been for some years the principal keeper of that light, a position he was obliged to resign, the close confinement affecting his health. Each of the men had been fifteen years in the service.

Smeaton tells of a shoemaker he met who had turned lighthousekeeeper at Eddystone because, he said, he did not like being confined to his work and found more freedom in a lighthouse than he could get at his last.

In 1870 the pay of an English light-keeper ranged from £52 to £72 per annum and these rates seem to be typical of the rest of Europe and America. Because of the low wages paid to keepers throughout the last century it is not unusual—or surprising—to find those who were stationed on mainland lights doubling as shoe-makers, tailors, etc., while in America we find them functioning as schoolteachers, justices of the peace and even clergymen. Because lighthouses are generally buildings of good order and set in picturesque surroundings, keepers had no difficulty in letting off rooms to summer visitors, although this practice was officially prohibited. In 1870 the Clyde Lighthouse Trustees discovered that some of their keepers were letting out the entire light-station as rooms, while they lived in near-by lodgings. Extra money could always be obtained in the form of gratuities from occasional visitors, for then, as now, the romance of the lighthouse was a steady draw to the tripper who (again, then as now) sometimes suffered a compulsion to leave his mark behind him. In 1870 the United States Lighthouse Board instructed its keepers that: 'Special care must be taken to prevent visitors from scratching their names or initials with diamond ornaments upon the glass of the lantern.'

Not all keepers of mainland stations were so well situated for social intercourse and the making of pocket money—some shore stations were as isolated as if they were on sea-swept rocks. This is demonstrated by a letter to the United States Lighthouse Board from the keeper of Bonita Point light off the Pacific coast:

There are no inhabitants within 5 miles of this point . . . from San Francisco to Point Bonita there is no direct communication but by chance, a sail boat may be procured at an expense of $5 and from $2 to $5 per barrel freight . . . my first assistant would only take the appointment by my agreeing to make our salaries equal, even then would only remain four months.

The authorities ignored this letter and, adding insult to injury, sent the keeper of Bonita Point a letter of their own:

You are charged with the firing of a 24-pounder gun placed at Bonita Point as a fog signal. . . . In the performance of your duties you will be governed by the following directions: to fire the gun every half-hour during fogs at the entrance of the Bay, whether they occur at night or in the day—the firing being made at the hours and half-hours of San Francisco mean time.

No doubt members of the Board were aware of the frequency of fogs at the Golden Gate, and if they also knew that the poor keeper was still without an assistant then they might well have been ashamed of themselves, when they received this reply:

I cannot find any person here to relieve me not five minutes, and I have been up three days and nights, had only two hours rest. . . . I was nearly used up. All the rest I would require in the 24 hours is two if I could only get it.

That he spent three days in that damp desolate place continually loading and firing a gun to give warning to shipping shows the keeper of Bonita Point to have been a man of great tenacity with a devotion to duty that came up to the standard demanded by the United States Lighthouse Board.

One maxim should ever be observed, namely, perfect regularity of exhibition of every signal from night to night and from year to year. A light, for example, which has been regularly visible from a tower, it may be for years, cannot be suffered to fail for a single hour, without danger of casualties of the most serious character.

Failures, in fact, are so rare as to be almost non-existent, but when caused through human agency they are severely dealt with. The letter below, written in 1908, is from the keeper of Akaroa (New Zealand) lighthouse:

Dear Sir,
    It is my sorrowful duty to report to you that on Saturday night last, I did let the machine stop revolving. In the last week I have been suffering toothache, very bad, and on Saturday I went into Akaroa for the mail and got two teeth out, from which I suffered very bad pain and distress. . . . I am very sorry, sir, that this has occurred and swear that this shall not happen again. I know that this is a serious crime and I had no more intention of going to sleep on watch than of flying. I do pray, sir, that you will overlook this, my first offence, and I swear that it shall be my last. My wife and I like the life and, sir, if you will overlook this. I shall spend the rest of my life in the service.

The keeper's offence was a grave one for it is far more serious to allow the lamp to stop revolving than it is to let it out altogether. No signal at all is better than an incorrect one. However, it is to be hoped that the keeper was forgiven and allowed to continue with the life he liked so much.
    A serious shipwreck occurred in April 1887 through the neglect of an assistant lighthouse keeper on Pointe d'Ailly. The principal keeper was off duty at the time and had gone to bed after instructing his wife to wake him if the prevailing mist on the sea grew any thicker. He was woken when the mist had turned into a dense fog, and noticing at once that the fog signal was not sounding he hurried to see what his assistant was doing. To his great dismay he found that instead of lighting the boiler fires upon the first onset of the fog, the assistant had done nothing and there was insufficient steam to work the siren. Efforts were, of course, at once made to get up steam, but before this could be done the cross-channel steamer *Victoria*, bound for Dieppe, ran directly into the rock and foundered. Thirty of the passengers and crew were lost.
    Shipwrecks near lighthouses usually occur in times of bad visibility, and it has often happened that the lifting of a fog has revealed to a keeper that there had been a disaster near by of which he was quite ignorant. Thus it was that the keeper of Skerries light was dining with his wife one day in the 1890s when a knock was heard at the lighthouse door. Being aware that he and his wife were the only inhabitants of that isolated rock, the keeper, with admirable *sang-froid*, ignored the noise and carried on with his dinner. After another disregarded tap the door opened and a stark naked Negro made his appearance, to the horror of the keeper and his wife who suspected

a visitation from the devil. In fact their caller was the only survivor of a ship that had foundered near by.

Women light-keepers were commonplace in Europe up to the close of the eighteenth century and they were extensively employed in America well into the twentieth. Maintained by the same woman for nearly fifty years, the harbour light at Michigan City became known as 'Miss Colfax's light'. The beacon was placed at the end of a long pier projecting into Lake Michigan and even when Miss Colfax had turned eighty years of age she could still be seen struggling along the pier against blustering winds, and sometimes gales, with a pan of hot lard-oil to fill the lamp. On one night in 1886 a particularly fierce gale was blowing and when Miss Colfax reached the foot of the pier she noticed it was shaking violently. The old lady did not hesitate but, reaching the end of the pier, she climbed the swaying tower and filled and trimmed the lamp. Having struggled back to the shore, she heard a great crash above the noise of the storm. The pier, tower, lamp and all, had disappeared into the sea.

A well-known woman keeper was Ida Lewis who kept Lime Rock lighthouse at Newport harbour where she lived for fifty-seven years. Her father had been appointed keeper when she was twelve, and after his death she tended the light for thirty-two years. During this time she saved thirteen people from drowning. The woman keeper of Angel Island light in San Francisco Bay, reporting a failure in the fog signal, wrote that she had 'struck the bell by hand for twenty hours and thirty-five minutes, until the fog lifted', and two days later 'stood all night on the platform outside and struck the bell with a nail hammer with all my might. The fog was very dense.'

In 1912 the lighthouse inspector of Staten Island received the following letter:

I am writing to you for a position as keeper in a lighthouse anywhere from New York to Portland, Maine. I am the daughter of a barge captain, and know much about the Sound and I also have a pal and we both are willing to do hard work and I know I would enjoy the lonesome life keeping the light a-burning. I know how to row and run an engine and steer a boat. I am afraid we will not get this position on account of us being girls but we shall wear trousers instead of skirts. I think that two strong girls like us could manage a lighthouse and keep a good log, and trusting that Uncle Sam will be good to us.

If the writer of this letter was successful in her application, which would seem doubtful, at least she would have had the advantage of choosing her 'pal' as her co-keeper. A dislike of the habits or even the face of an enforced companion can cause misery in the confines of a lighthouse, while an outright quarrel could make life almost unbearable for even the most tolerant of individuals. The lighthouse engineer Robert Stevenson wrote:

The light-keeper occupies a place apart among men. . . . These usually pass their time by the pleasant human expedient of quarrelling; and sometimes, I am assured, not one of the three is on speaking terms with any other. On shore stations, which on the Scottish coast are sometimes hardly less isolated, the usual number is two, a principal and an assistant. The principal is dissatisfied with the assistant, or perhaps the assistant keeps pigeons, and the principal wants the water from the roof. Their wives and families are with them, living cheek by jowl. The children quarrel; Jockie hits Jimsie in the eye, and the mothers make haste to mingle in the dissension. Perhaps there is trouble about a broken dish; perhaps Mrs Assistant is more highly born than Mrs Principal and gives herself airs; and the men are drawn in and the servants presently follow.

The log of Akaroa lighthouse gives a first-hand account of one of these dramas. Written in an immaculate copperplate hand and dated 11 July 1883, the principal keeper records:

The assistant keeper made a complaint to me that my son had stolen two eggs from his foulhouse. On endeavouring to find out from him if he actually saw my son take the eggs, both he and his wife were most insolent and abusive to me, saying I was a wretch, the same as all the rest of them in the light service, from the highest to the lowest;[1] but he admitted he did not actually see the boy take the eggs.

Nine days later a further instalment appears:

About noon today the assistant keeper's wife came to my house and said she wanted to have some words with me. I said I did not, and if it concerned her eggs, her husband was the person I should hear, not her. She would not be denied and I said, 'Please, Mrs, go out of my house'. She would not go and I went around to see her husband and asked him to take his wife out of my house. He told me he would not do any such thing. I then told him, that if he did not get her away, I would have to put her out. He said: 'You dare to, and out of the service you shall go'. I then took hold of his arm and said: 'Do come'. He then assaulted me and in self defence I had to use violence also. I went back to my house and found his wife pouring out angry words to my wife, who was in tears, and my children terrified. I put the assistant's wife, gently but firmly out of my house. Then they made a combined attack on me, and to avoid them, I retreated into my house, his wife crying out after me: 'What about the fire? Who set fire to the paraffin?'

Another incident between two keepers is recorded in the same log in 1890 and if they were the same two keepers who had fought over the two eggs, as seems likely, the feud had continued for seven years:

At 3 a.m. I called the assistant's attention to the light, which was a very inferior one. I pointed the fault to him, but he appeared to resent my authority of inter-

[1] This would appear to be a piece of embroidery inserted into the story by the principal keeper to anger the inspector when he read the log.

ference. He told me I was all blow. One word led to another, and running up to me he shook his fist in my face, saying, let it be a bloody caution to me if I made him mad.

It is not surprising that friction existed among men confined together in isolated or wave-swept stations, in particular where keepers were unable to put more than a few yards between themselves. In such stations as Eddystone, Rothersand or Minot's Ledge, for instance, the only retreat from the rooms of the tower is the outside gallery which, windy and confined, is hardly the best place for a walk.

Smeaton relates that while on a visit to Eddystone he learned that the two keepers there had not spoken to each other for a month, and goes on to remark that candidates for the position of light-keeper must be naturally morose and perhaps slightly misanthropic!

Apart from their handicrafts the light-keepers of the nineteenth century had little else to occupy their leisure time. The Literature for Lighthouses Mission supplied small libraries which were changed with each relief and which consisted of '. . . a Bible and Prayerbook and books suitable for persons of their class'. By the end of the century most isolated stations were connected to the nearest town by telephone over which the newspapers were read to the keepers each morning. Fishing, of course, has always been popular among keepers, and where it is not possible to cast a line clear of the rocks, kite-fishing is resorted to. In 1893 the three European keepers of Turnabout lighthouse, off the China coast, took a boat out to fish for crabs. Unfortunately the boat capsized, drowning one of the men. The other two had to swim around for two hours while arguing the price of rescue with the local fishermen who had rowed out to assist them. It was, perhaps, an attempt to catch fish which led to a mystery that will always remain a classic of the sea and of lighthouses in particular.

Standing twenty-two miles off the Isle of Lewis among the Hebridean Islands is a cluster of isolated rocks known as the Seven Hunters, or the Flannen Islands, on one of the highest of which stands a tower erected by David and Charles Stevenson. It is so desolate a spot in winter, frequented by so little shipping, that the light may flash heedlessly for nights on end. On Boxing Day, 1900, the relief tender made its fortnightly visit to the Flannen light but the crew were surprised that, on approaching, the usual signals were absent; so was the appearance of the keepers who invariably came down to the landing stage to greet them. Now thoroughly puzzled, the crew of the tender made their way inside the lighthouse and found it completely deserted, while a search made of the rock yielded no trace of the missing keepers. An examination of the log showed the last entry as having been made at 4 a.m. nearly a week previously; the lamp had not been abandoned but had burned out of oil. Many sensational rumours were circulated and even published purporting to explain the mystery, including the favourite lighthouse story of sudden insanity and murder, but there was not the slightest sign on the rock or in the tower that could explain the sudden disappearance of three men. It must be assumed that one of them went out onto the rock and was swept into the sea by the violent storm that was then blowing. His companions in attempting to rescue him were also caught by the sea and swept in after him.

Even though most isolated light-stations are now equipped with television sets, the modern keeper spends most of his leisure time in much the same way as did his predecessors. In fact he probably spends less time gazing at the television screen than does the average landlubber. Much of his time is spent in such occupations as model-making, painting, rug-making and basketry; in addition the isolated lighthouse makes an ideal place for study. Many keepers take correspondence courses in various subjects—one keeper recently became a qualified solicitor in his spare time. Lighthouse authorities receive a steady flow of applications from students who want to spend a limited time as a lighthouse keeper in order to prepare for an examination. These requests, of course, cannot be granted.

The conditions of entry and service as a keeper to Trinity House lighthouse service are fairly typical. Applicants must be between eighteen and thirty-two years of age and the first listed requirement is that they must be dentally fit—a very wise rule, one would agree, at the thought of being marooned on Eddystone with a raging toothache. On appointment the recruit spends four weeks at Harwich taking instruction in the various types of equipment: explosive fog signals; morse and semaphore signalling; cookery; first aid; radio telephony, etc. He then goes to a shore lighthouse where he receives further instruction in the handling of equipment. He is next employed in relief duties until such time as he is appointed to a particular lighthouse. It is likely that his first permanent station will be one of the old isolated towers, it being a logical deduction that if a man can prove himself satisfactory and can himself stand life in the confined and monotonous surroundings of a sea-swept tower such as Wolf Rock, that if he does not allow his companions to get on his nerves and does not himself get on theirs, then he should be perfectly happy in the service when his turn comes to be posted ashore. In practice only about half the entrants stay the course of the first year—the others return to more prosaic occupations. Keepers on rock stations are given one month's shore leave for every two spent on duty in addition to their annual leave. As has always been the custom, the keepers each provide their own food and inform the cook of the day what they require for each meal. The deep-freeze refrigerator must have been an even greater boon to lighthouse keepers than the television.

A few years ago one Edward Wood went to Bishop's Rock to make a Christmas Day broadcast for the B.B.C. While he was there he marvelled at the 'cheerfulness and philosophic calm' with which the keepers carried out their duties. Mr Wood had intended his visit to Bishop's Rock to last three days, but during his stay the weather turned nasty. Four weeks later he managed to get ashore. At the time of writing this chapter I learn that the relief for Bishop's Rock is three weeks overdue. This aspect of light-house keeping has not changed since Winstanley's times.

19

Sea-lights and Automation

I T IS ONE of the paradoxes of the 'technological age' that the further
the science of automation advances the more difficult it seems to be to
obtain labour. This difficulty results in increasing wages—a tendency
that spurs the development of even more automation. In no other sphere
is this process more apparent than in the lighthouse service. A few years
ago no lighthouse authority was without a long waiting list of would-be
light-keepers[1] but now, in the western world at any rate, it has become very
difficult to recruit men to a career that will probably begin with long
periods spent in isolation. As a consequence much effort has been put into
the development of remote controlled and automated equipment as well as
new light sources that do not demand the constant attention of an oil-
light. The new tower at Dungeness is lighted by a xenon high-pressure arc
lamp, a form of illumination originally developed by the film industry in
1961 for the showing of coloured motion pictures. The light is produced
by a powerful electric arc in an inert gas-filled bulb of quartz. The small-
ness and brilliance of the light source makes it possible to employ a small
optical system. In the case of Dungeness, the lamp is contained in a lens of
only 500 mm diameter and gives a light of 300,000 candle power. In 1963
a 2-kilowatt xenon arc lamp was tested that gave 4,000,000 candle power.
Another type of lamp using xenon gas is the xenon flash discharge which
works on the same principle as a neon lamp but which uses xenon gas
instead of neon.

On Oak Island (New York City) there is a very fine lighthouse with two
lighting systems, one of low intensity and the other, consisting of mercury
arc lamps, of high intensity. Both systems comprise four commercial type

[1] See Appendix A.

searchlights and both sets of four, mounted on the same shaft, are electrically revolved. The four low-intensity searchlights are each lit by a 1-kilowatt filament lamp giving a total of 1,400,000 candle power. Four miles away from the lighthouse is a small monitor lamp and as long as this lamp is visible from the lighthouse the low-intensity system is kept in operation. When visibility is reduced to the point where the monitor light cannot be seen, the high-intensity system is brought into use. This consists of a 2·5-kilowatt mercury short-arc lamp in each of four 36-inch searchlights, and gives a beam of no less than 14,000,000 candle power that is visible for nineteen miles.

A great deal of research was carried out in the 1960s into new sources of power for sea-lights. In particular, experiments have been carried out in the use of solar batteries to supply electricity to low-powered lights. A sun-powered light was established in Crossness beacon on the river Thames and it has worked without trouble for over two years. Another source of power at present under development is known as RIPPLE—Radio Isotopic Prolonged Life Equipment; it is, as its name suggests, a nuclear battery.

In December 1969 Trinity House took possession of their first 'Lanby' buoy to replace the Shambles lightship. Lanby (Large Automatic Navigational Buoy) is a fully automatic unmanned buoy of 40-foot diameter weighing 84 tons, and its running cost is about 90 per cent less than the £29,000 a year that is required to maintain a lightship. Its navigational aids consist of a main light 40 feet above sea-level with a range of sixteen miles, a powerful fog signal, radio beacons and meteorological data-reporting equipment, power being supplied by three 5-kilowatt diesel generating sets. The buoy's operation is monitored every thirty minutes by the control station on shore. In the event of a failure, emergency services operate automatically and the nature of the fault is relayed to the shore station. Shore control can carry out forty separate checks on the equipment and can control twenty-two operations on the buoy. Lanby can be moored in up to 300 feet of water and can withstand winds of up to 100 m.p.h., waves of up to 40 feet and currents of up to 7 knots.

For the monitoring of unattended lighthouses a most ingenious piece of equipment has been developed that passes verbal information to a keeper stationed ashore. It consists of a radio transmitter and a vocal recording of every conceivable piece of information that may be required by the keeper on the state of affairs existing in the lighthouse. The keeper may make a specific enquiry by dialling a code or, in the case of a fault occurring, the lighthouse automatically contacts the keeper. In effect, the keeper carries on a conversation with his lighthouse, for in response to a message received from it he may dial one of a series of codes which may, for example, stop or start the light or the fog signal or replace a faulty piece of equipment.

Microphones, placed at strategic points in the lighthouse, enable the keeper to listen to the running of any item of equipment or to check on the performance of the fog signal.

With these advances in lighthouse automation and with others that will doubtless follow, it might appear that the isolated light-keeper will soon become extinct. In fact this cannot be in the foreseeable future. Most of the old granite towers—Eddystone, Wolf Rock, Skerryvore, Rothersand, Heaux de Bréhat, to name but a few—are still in use. Although they are not suitable for automatic installations these sturdy towers are as structurally sound as ever they were, and there are no plans for replacing them.

Lighthouses that are inaccessible in bad weather will always have their resident keepers; for it is during this bad weather that the light is most needed and it is when conditions make the rock inaccessible that it is imperative that any breakdown of the light be attended to immediately.

Although the future will see a great increase in the number of radio aids to shipping, it seems likely that the flashing light will always be used as a warning to mariners, for in the last resort these lights, with their primary and emergency sources of power, are the most reliable and unmistakable signs of danger and guidance at sea.

A lighthouse intended for the Dominican city of Santo Domingo has been designed primarily as a symbol and only secondly as a navigational aid. Santo Domingo, founded in 1502 as Ciudad Trujillo, is the oldest European city in the Americas and in its cathedral lies the body of Christopher Columbus. The idea for the lighthouse was first put forward as long ago as 1852 when a Dominican historian proposed the building of a light-tower that would also serve as the tomb of Columbus. Throughout the rest of the nineteenth century, and well into the twentieth, committees were formed and resolutions passed on the project but nothing of a practical nature was done until, in 1927, an international competition was arranged to choose a design. This was won by a Scottish architect, J. L. Greave, with a design for a huge building, mainly in the form of a recumbent cross and containing a chapel, a museum, a library and a tomb for the remains of Columbus, as well as a light-tower. The structure will be low and massive as 'it is intended to be all-enduring'. The lighthouse is not intended to be merely a memorial to Columbus but 'as one of the great gestures of the ages it is a monument to glorify an ideal—his ideal and our ideal. The innate urge to an unknown end. The urge that we call progress, and the unknown end that over the Christian World is known as God and symbolized by the Cross.' In style the design follows no specific architectural idiom although it hints at the pre-Columbian architecture of America, the great Pharos of Alexandria and the architecture of the modern movement. Carved over the whole surface of the mass will be the names and deeds of the men and women who have contributed to the world's progress.

The scheme again lay dormant, this time for twenty years, until in 1946 it was approved by the General Assembly of U.N.O., the twenty-one Republics of America agreeing to contribute towards the cost of building. Here the matter still rests. One day, no doubt, the Columbus Memorial Lighthouse will be built and very impressive it might well be—'A single idea carried out on a magnificent scale. The New World signed with the sign of the cross.' As a 'symbol of progress' I, for one, prefer the slender form of an old rock tower—a symbol not only of progress but of watchfulness, courage and humanity. Without the sea-beacon—be it bonfire, tallow candle, oil lamp or xenon arc—sea-borne commerce would still be groping in the dark. If the sea-routes of the world were opened by the heroic explorers of the fifteenth, sixteenth and seventeenth centuries then it was the builders and keepers of lighthouses who made it possible for mankind to develop those routes to the full.

Appendix A

LIFE AS A LIGHTHOUSE KEEPER, written by a light-keeper under the Northern Lights Commissioners, *circa* 1900.[1]

An application for getting into the Lighthouse Service must in the first place be made to the Secretary by some responsible person known personally to the applicant, who may be afterwards interviewed by one of the Officers of the Board. If the applicant is supposed to be efficient, and passes a medical examination, and is between twenty and twenty-five years of age, his name will be placed on the Applicants' List. There are always a large number on this list, many of whom never get an appointment, owing to the few vacancies occurring in the year. Sailors and mechanical tradesmen get the preference. Yearly in October those selected are called up to Edinburgh to undergo a simple examination in reading, writing and arithmetic, and a strict examination by a doctor. If he passes through this ordeal successfully, he is sent to be instructed in the duties of a Lighthouse Keeper, viz.: six weeks at a Dioptric or Lens Light, and six weeks at a Catoptric or Reflector Light, with fog signal duties to learn at one or both stations. After he gets through these routine duties, his name will be placed on the Expectant List to wait his turn for an appointment, but should he attain the age of thirty years before his turn comes round, his name is removed from the list.

The duties which devolve on Lightkeepers are many and various, and require constant attention and vigilance. The most important are the night duties, which commence at lighting time (sunset), when the lamps are lit and must be kept burning brightly till sunrise the following morning. The night is divided into watches of about three or four hours, according to the number of men at the station. Most lighthouses are of a revolving character. At a lens station the lamp is fixed on a table in the centre of the lens, which revolves round the lamp by means of a machine. The lens apparatus are differently constructed so as to distinguish the character of the lights in the same district.

[1] Reprinted from an undated issue of *The Lightkeeper*, journal of the Literature to Lighthouses Mission.

The kind of machine used is just clockwork on a large scale; sometimes the weight is five cwt. A similar small machine is used for pumping the oil up to the lamp. This machine pumps up far more oil than the lamp consumes, but the overflow runs back to the fountain again. Both machines run for about one hour, when the Keeper on watch must wind them up again, and so on through the night. He has also to keep the lantern clear of sweat inside, and of snow on the outside whenever snow falls; and perhaps the most arduous job a Lightkeeper has to do is to go outside the lantern in a gale of wind to clean the snow off. Sometimes he has to hold on with both hands for fear of being thrown off; and he may not be a quarter of an hour in when he has to go out again. He has also to keep constant lookout, especially in rough weather, for any vessel which may be in distress. Whenever such occurs it must be immediately reported to the nearest coastguard or lifeboat station. A number of lighthouses are now connected by telephone for this purpose, which can be used day or night. Rockets are kept at some others for summoning lifeboats, and the International Code of Signals for using through the day, but only for reporting casualties at sea.

The Keeper on duty has to make readings of the barometer and thermometer, and to mark down the state of the weather and different directions of the wind, which must be written in a book for the purpose, returns of which are sent to the Office and Meteorological Society monthly. He has also to note every light in the district, and to write it in another book, whether seen or not seen as the case may be. If a Lightkeeper, through his negligence, allows a light to become extinguished, or a revolving light to become stationary, he is dismissed the service, and forfeits all claim to pension, however long he may have served.

A Lightkeeper's daily routine commences at 9 a.m. in the light room, trimming the lamps and cleaning the lens and prisms; the reflectors (the face of which is of finely polished silver) must be particularly cleaned and polished by commencing in the centre and working with a circular motion outwards. A little rouge is used on the chamois skins for the reflectors. Visitors to a lighthouse often wonder at their brightness and beauty, and ask what they are cleaned with. Then the machines have to be rubbed and oiled, brass work polished, and the whole place dusted down. These duties usually occupy both Keepers from an hour to three hours daily in the light room. The outside premises have also to be kept in order. All woodwork and ironwork is painted every summer; lighthouses are so exposed to sea-spray that this is absolutely necessary. Tower dwelling-houses and boundary walls are lime-washed annually. Besides a little gardening, the above duties roughly forms the Lighthouse Keeper's daily routine. Paraffin oil is used at mostly all the first-class lights, gas at a few, and the electric light at one. The oil is much finer than the ordinary shop oil; it is also safer, the flashing point being about 150 dg. The consumption of oil is very great—a six-inch wick lamp burns a gallon every two hours. Now and again some improvement is made in the system of the lighthouse illumination, the latest being the substitution of a small burner of about two inches diameter, and using a mantle—or, as it is called, the incandescent light—the gas of which gives the flame. This invention has several advantages: less oil is required, a better light is given at less expense, and less labour is involved to the crews of the steam tenders, and to the Light-keepers in carrying it up a high winding stair, often upwards of 100 feet.

At each station there is a man appointed styled the Occasional Keeper; he must be a resident near the lighthouse if possible, and is instructed in the duties of that station. In the event of a Keeper being absent, or off duty through illness, the 'Occasional' is called in to do the light-room duty.

At island stations there is a boatman and boat-crew appointed to attend the lighthouse, who have to make a trip to the lighthouse with letters, provisions, and sometimes with water, once every week or fortnight, when the weather permits. At island stations the boatman is communicated with by signals in case of distress or when assistance is urgently wanted.

A Lightkeeper on appointment gets £54 15s ($273), rising about £3 ($15) every five years to £76 ($380), the latter amount being only obtained after about twenty-seven years' service. In addition, we have a free house, partly furnished, with coal and oil, and a suit of clothes every year.

Appendix B

Extract from *Lightkeepers Manual, circa* 1900.

DUTIES CONNECTED WITH THE LIGHTING

Morning duties

Every morning, at daybreak, the keeper should ascend to the lantern and proceed with his duties, as follows:
If the apparatus is revolving, the motor-weight of the clock-work will be entirely wound up and fastened, the work stopped, and the wheel which communicates motion thrown out of gear.
If the lamp be mounted in the apparatus on a movable table, that table will be lowered.
If the apparatus be hoisted on a bracket, it will be lowered until it rests on the service-table intended to receive it.
The light will be extinguished, observing the precautions mentioned above, and the chimney will be wiped with care within and without, then wrapped in a dry cloth and placed where it will be free from dust.
The lamp will be removed from the apparatus, and, if it be a constant-level one, placed on its service-stand.
The apparatus will be dusted with the feather-brush, and wiped with a soft linen cloth that is free from dust. If any part be spotted with oil, it will be washed with a little spirits of wine.
The apparatus will then be covered with its linen cover. The glass of the lantern will be carefully wiped within and without, and, if necessary, cleaned with whiting, or, if necessary, with polishing-rouge.
If the lantern be provided with curtains, they will be hung in place.
The service-table, the pedestal and the interior part of the lantern wall will be dusted, and the staircase swept.
This done, the lamp will be taken into the store-room and weighed to ascertain the amount of oil consumed during the night; then it will be emptied, and the oil poured into the strainer.
The oil which has fallen into the drip-cup during the night will be placed

in the vessel kept for leavings, and will be reserved for the use of the keeper.

The burner will be cleaned with care within and without. The burned oil attached to its edges will be removed with the triangular scraper; a bottle-brush will be passed through the interior air-tube, and the outside wiped with a linen cloth.

The buttons of the lamps burning schist oil will be carefully wiped.

The body of the lamp will be wiped and cleaned. Finally, the lamp will be filled, the wick trimmed or replaced, and the lamp again set in the apparatus, so that every thing may be ready for lighting up at evening.

Care will be taken that the spare lamp, which should be in the light-room, is in a serviceable condition. If the apparatus by sideral, two extra wick-carriers, provided with their wicks, should be ready to be placed in the lamp.

A can filled with strained oil will be carried up into the lantern, or placed at the foot of the pedestal, to be poured into the spare lamp if required.

Evening duties

Every evening at sunset, the keeper will ascend into the lantern, after having provided himself with a lighted lucerne.

If the morning duties have been regularly performed, the following state of things will appear:

The lamp of the apparatus will be in place and ready to be lighted; its chimney will be in the service-closet, as will the extra lamp, the burner, the two chimneys and the service-box containing the various utensils. The weight of the revolving machinery in lights varied by flashes will be found entirely wound up, the main wheel held by its bolt, and the wheels which communicate the motion out of gear.

The cover of the apparatus will be removed, and the lighting commenced half an hour after sunset, so that the light may be at its full brilliancy by nightfall, and in this operation the directions just given will be followed.

If the apparatus be on rollers, it will be placed in the position it ought to occupy during the night, and kept there by means of a stop-bolt.

At nightfall the curtains of the lantern will be removed, folded and placed in the service-closet, if the apparatus be contained in a fixed lantern. If the apparatus be in a movable lantern, this will be hoisted to the full height of the scaffold or the pedestal.

If the apparatus shows a variable light, the revolving machinery will be put in motion immediately after lighting. To do this it is sufficient to gear the cog-wheels, withdraw the bolt of the main wheel, and remove the pin which holds the motor-weight.

When the cold is so intense that colza oil will congeal, the following precautions will be taken before lighting:

1st. An hour before sunset the lamp will be taken down and emptied, and the oil heated until too hot for the hand to be held in it; after which the burner will be plunged in it and kept there some moments; it will then be restored to place, and the oil poured back into the lamp.

2nd. The heater will be got ready and put in place. From April 1st to October 1st, the light will be visited by the keeper at least once every night, and during the remainder of the year twice every night, and oftener, if from any cause there may be reason to fear that the light may go out or decrease much in intensity.

These nocturnal visits will be made during the summer at about midnight; in the winter at about 11 p.m. and 2 a.m. At each visit the keeper will carry the lighting-lamp.

When the keeper sees that the wick is charred, and should be trimmed or cleaned, he will proceed as follows, according to the kind of lamp.

If it be a constant-level or mechanical lamp, he will immediately replace it with the spare lamp, having filled this with oil and lighted it outside the apparatus. If it be a lamp belonging to sideral apparatus, he will remove the wick-carrier and replace it with one of the spare ones, which he will immediately light. All these operations should be performed as quickly as possible.

Having properly placed the new lamp, the one taken from the apparatus will be set on the service-table, and then trimmed so that it may be returned to place if necessary.

The piston of the moderator lamp should be wound up at each visit.

When the apparatus is lighted by a schist-oil lamp with a cistern below, care should be taken to change the service-lamp toward the middle of the night, lighting the extra lamp before putting it in place. In no case should oil be poured into a schist-oil lamp while it is lighted.

Bibliography

ADAM, W. H. D. *Lighthouses and Lightships* (London, 1870)
ADAMSON, H. C. *Keepers of the Lights* (New York, 1955)
BANISTER, T. R. *The Coastwise Lights of China* (1932)
BARRETT, C. R. B. *The Trinity House of Deptford Strond* (London, 1893)
BLAKE, C. *Lighthouse Management* (1861)
BOWEN, J. P. *British Lighthouses* (London, 1947)
COLLINS, F. A. *Sentinels Along Our Coast* (New York, 1922)
CONKLIN, I. *Guideposts of the Sea* (New York, 1939)
CROWNSHIELD, M. *All Among the Lighthouses* (Boston, 1886)
DOUGLASS, W. T. *The New Eddystone Lighthouse* (1883)
EDWARDS, E. P. *The Eddystone Lighthouses* (London, 1882)
FINDLAY, A. J. *A Description of the Lighthouses of the World* (1861)
FLOHERTY, J. J. *Sentries of the Sea* (Philadelphia, 1942)
HARDY, W. J. *Lighthouses* (London, 1895)
HEAP, D. P. *Ancient and Modern Lighthouses* (Boston, 1889)
HOLMES, F. M. *Stories of Lighthouses and Their Builders* (London, 1896)
LEA, J. *Danger Signals* (London, 1910)
MacCORMICK, W. H. *The Modern Book of Lighthouses* (London, 1936)
MAJDALANY, F. *The Red Rocks of Eddystone* (London, 1959)
MILLS, R. *The American Pharos* (1832)
OWEN, F. C. *Sentinels of the Sea* (New York, 1926)
PUTNAM, G. R. *Lighthouses and Lightships of the United States* (Boston, 1933)
——————. *Sentinel of the Coasts* (New York, 1922)
SMEATON, J. *Narrative of the Building of the Eddystone Lighthouse* (1792)
SMILES, S. *Lives of the Engineers* (London, 1904)
SNOW, E. R. *Famous Lighthouses of America* (New York, 1955)
STEVENSON, A. *Account of the Bell Rock Lighthouse* (1824)
——————. *Account of the Skerryvore Lighthouse* (1848)
STEVENSON, D. A. *The World's Lighthouses Before 1820* (London, 1959)
STEVENSON, R. *The Bell Rock Lighthouse* (London, 1931)
——————. (edited by D. A. Stevenson). *English Lighthouse Tours* (London, 1946)
STEVENSON, T. *Lighthouse Construction* (London, 1881)
TAIT, T. R. *The Early History of Lighthouses* (Edinburgh, 1902)

TALBOT, F. A. *Lightships and Lighthouses* (London, 1913)

WESTON, R. H. *Letters and Documents Relative to the Eddystone Lighthouse* (1811)

WILLOUGHBY, M. F. *Lighthouses of New England* (Boston, 1929)

WRIGHT, W. H. K. *The Eddystone Lighthouses* (Plymouth, 1884)

WRYDE, J. S. *British Lighthouses* (London, 1913)

————— . *The United States Lighthouse Service* (London, 1915)

Index

Index